MW00862272

# Movement and Meaning THE LANDSCAPES OF HOERR SCHAUDT

# Movement and Meaning THE LANDSCAPES OF HOERR SCHAUDT

Written with Douglas Brenner Foreword by Laurence Booth

The Monacelli Press

# Contents

For PETER LINDSAY SCHAUDT (1959–2015)

The thing that's important is not something called design;
it's how you live, it's life itself. Design really comes from that.
You cannot separate what you do from your life.

–DANIEL URBAN KILEY

# Foreword

Laurence Booth

I first met Peter Schaudt when, as a young, aspiring architect, he became a student of mine at the University of Illinois at Chicago. I was teaching a studio on the design of a Midwestern town. Peter delivered an exceptional scheme for the town hall: well organized, thought-through, and expressing a quiet authority. When Peter later shifted his sights to landscape architecture, no one was surprised that he went on to Harvard and a Rome Prize. Peter eventually returned to Chicago and opened his own small studio, surviving on a few large commissions.

Doug Hoerr seemed to appear out of the blue—or so it seemed to Chicagoans unaware of his landscape architecture degree from Purdue, his decade in design/build, and his two-year apprenticeship with leading British garden designers. Chicago has the noble tradition of a few talented landscape architects, like Jens Jensen and Alfred Caldwell, who were happy with a limited palette of plants and harsh winters. In 1994, when Doug's Michigan Avenue plantings went in, people instantly realized that another singular landscape talent had arrived. I soon got to know Doug and always tried to get him on our project teams.

In 2008, Doug and Peter announced the merger of their competing landscape architecture firms. This news was noted at the time as a bit unusual. How, observers wondered, could these two extraordinary, and very different, designers—Doug's craft honed by hands-on expertise, Peter's burnished by academia—merge and work together?



The partnership worked as an enriching experience for both principals as they built a team of forty staff architects who enjoyed creative, thoughtful, and demanding professional lives. Peter gave Doug an understanding of large-scale public design, while Doug brought Peter a fresh focus on intimacy, sensory appeal, and the unexpected.

Peter approached landscapes deliberately, through a process integrating deep knowledge with keen analysis. Doug is a landscape architect from the "ground up" who intuitively envisions landscapes complete with the texture, form, and color of plants and other materials. So while the two did not work arm in arm on individual projects, they together created a firm culture dedicated to craft through tight attention to detail, constructability, and durability.

Like an electric field formed by paired charges, Hoerr Schaudt became an extraordinary practice energized to excel, synthesizing biophilia and urbanity. As an architect, I have enjoyed and benefited from collaboration with these designers inspired by Nature who are also intent on focusing the entire human experience of a place.

Peter's legacy lives on in the extraordinarily creative work of Hoerr Schaudt, as Doug continues the energy and quality of the public and private projects illustrated in this remarkable book.

# Apprentices and Masters

The dynamic meeting of minds that animates everything Hoerr Schaudt builds and plants has produced an uncommonly diverse portfolio. Exuberance and restraint, spontaneity and reflection, romance and pragmatism, memory and anticipation all figure in the mix. Anybody who tries to pin one neat label onto this protean force will find it a moving target.



A sense of movement—physical, intellectual, and emotional—unites otherwise disparate designs by Doug Hoerr and the late Peter Schaudt. For them, nature abhors inertia, and a landscape asserts its life-enhancing power when it inspires exploration and discovery. Structure and horticulture act as equal partners in shaping those adventures, whether the setting is a family backyard, a public plaza, a university campus, or a corporate park.

The route traveled may be a rustic path or a city street. The view ahead may be framed by an allée or a windshield. With subtle guidance, the eye that delights in possessing every square inch of a private terrace can freely "borrow" a next-door neighbor's treetops or a skyscraper spire across town. Roof decks transformed into prairies become plein-air artworks for anonymous onlookers. When a garden yearns to meet a lake or river, the gardener acts as matchmaker. Facades, windows, doors, and furniture become props for indoor-outdoor dramas, even in places where winter directs the show. New earth works give a contemporary edge to age-old landforms, and children safely romp in a traffic circle.

From the start of Doug Hoerr and Peter Schaudt's partnership, their work has redrawn conventional boundaries of style and scale to meet the functional challenges posed by specific sites and programs. "Doug and I refuse to become serial designers," Schaudt told me when I met with him and Hoerr in their Chicago office. "Our only dogma is not having a dogma." That versatility springs in part from a pragmatism that both men attribute to their regional milieu: Hoerr grew up in Indiana farm country, Schaudt in suburban Chicago. "Maybe it's the Midwest in us," Hoerr said, "that we never expect the people hiring us to go, 'Have at it! Do what you want.'" Schaudt added: "Clients here are sophisticated, smart, and straightforward—and they expect good value. Our brutal winters and hot summers are a boot camp for designers, so even when a project takes us far away, we never lose sight of durability and practicality."

The two men's contrasting yet surprisingly complementary design methods—Schaudt's collaborative, Hoerr's more individualistic—are also embedded in personal history. As an architecture student Schaudt thrived on camaraderie in studio courses, but academic feuds over the ascendance of postmodernism disheartened him: "I felt it was trivial—it had nothing to do with society as a whole. I wanted to work with environments that mattered to the people who use them." Studio projects on Chicago parks, a merit-award-winning entry in the Washington Vietnam Veterans Memorial competition, and encounters with the work of landscape architect Dan Kiley amounted to a professional epiphany.

Hoerr's postgraduate employment at a large design-build concern in Peoria, Illinois, developed his skills at construction, project-management, and business. He also shouldered major responsibilities for design, even though the only time for project sketches and plans came at the end of long workdays driving tractors and tree spades, laying stone walls and brick patios, directing work crews and tagging truckloads of plants. "But after nine years," he said, "I was eager to move on and apply what I'd learned in Peoria to becoming the best landscape architect I could be, by any measure." Hoerr's agrarian background impelled him to pursue his hands-on version of an MA in horticulture and design: a two-year immersion in the art and craft of English gardening. "It was the 1980s, and everybody agreed that England was the place to go. Had I wanted to learn blues, I would have gone to Chicago and tracked down Buddy Guy."

"Peter and I realize that we owe a debt to those who taught us," Hoerr went on. "We were fortunate to have apprenticed with true masters." Hoerr found his English mentors at age thirty-two, working in the private gardens of eminent British plantsmen and designers. Beth Chatto taught him the importance of cultivating plants in conditions akin to their native habitats. "I suddenly just *got it*," he recalled. "How could a curry plant ever be happy in Illinois loam, when it naturally grows in cracks in volcanic loam?" Garden writer Christopher Lloyd chuckled over Hoerr's lament that he could never replicate

Doug Hoerr, TOP, tends the trial garden of English nurseryman Adrian Bloom, in 1989. Peter Schaudt, BOTTOM, shares a laugh with Dan Kiley in 1987.

the nonstop bloom of a proper herbaceous border back home—and his disbelief at the cannas and zinnias heretically mingling with the Englishman's perennials. "You Americans are so uptight," Lloyd said. "Perennials, annuals—they're all plants. It isn't cheating to put them together." John Brookes opened Hoerr's eyes to the concept of outdoor rooms and, more profoundly, to his true vocation: a designer who uses plants as a creative medium. "And that's why later, on Michigan Avenue" Hoerr told me, "I could make annuals look like drifts of perennials. It's why I can create the look of a prairie, but layer in the occasional *nonnative* for richer color and texture. We can put together the distinctive bones of a project—its shapes and patterns—and then infuse it with actual plant material."

Although Peter Schaudt's apprenticeship in Dan Kiley's four-man office lasted only two years, its influence on his own career was lifelong. "Dan taught me that design is a struggle, a humbling process of not knowing. It shouldn't latch onto a preconceived idea. But it also leads to a joyous discovery." Schaudt also loved collaborating with architects: "Every one of them has a different way of solving problems. Playing a part in how they get to the finished building is the real fun for me. If either of us has a better idea than the other, we're going to run with it." None of the many honors Schaudt received pleased him more than the American Institute of Architects 2011 Collaborative Achievement Award.

The graceful understatement and geometric logic of Schaudt's landscape designs express his admiration for architect Louis I. Kahn as effectively as they evoke Dan Kiley's minimalist aesthetic. A connoisseur of trees, like Kiley, Schaudt valued nature as a key collaborator. He would pace back and forth at a nursery, pondering the pros and cons of a hybrid elm versus a Redmond linden for a particular job. But his regard for green beauty and sustainability also extended beyond the outer reaches of the plant kingdom. Schaudt interrupted his explanation of water filters at Uptown Normal— "my favorite project of all I have worked on"—to exclaim, "I love the algae stain on the concrete. A biological event is happening right in front of us!"



Embracing the infinite changes wrought by time—both fortuitous and planned—has been Hoerr Schaudt's credo from the founding of the firm. Not that the designers aren't prepared to transplant mature trees with Brobdingnagian root balls for clients intent on instant gratification. More than once Hoerr has been advised, "Don't plant any green bananas for me." Successful collaborations with eminent architects such as Booth Hansen, Peter Gluck+, Perkins+ Will, and Robert A.M. Stern reinforce mutual respect. Nonetheless, Schaudt said, "I sometimes tease architects, 'You guys have got it made. From the minute you're building's done, it's all there. It's static. But our work is ever-changing.'"

Hoerr expands: "An architect can specify any size I-beam, but we can't just tell the contractor, 'Give me a really nice six-inch-caliper oak with furrowed bark that branches out just so.' No, you've got to go find it, because every oak has a different personality. Every selection has to build on the whole. It's all interconnected." The same principle holds for the hardscape that's just as essential to the totality of a Hoerr Schaudt scheme. With painstaking considerations—from stepping-stone to boulder, fencepost to pergola—momentum builds. —D.B.

A path meandering across a suburban backyard feels worlds apart from an avenue bustling between downtown skyscrapers. But in Hoerr Schaudt's design atlas, all routes lead to the same conclusion: Getting there should be half the fun, no matter how brief the itinerary or how big the party. "If you can delight the one, you can delight the many," Doug Hoerr says. Peter Schaudt held the belief that a fulfilling passage through space and time, creatively plotted by structure and horticulture, defies measurement by scale or program alone.



At the Renker residence, for example, a feeling of boundless serenity has been conjured up on less than an acre of California desert. Exquisite trees, ancient sculptures, and axial vistas elevate every walk from driveway to pool into a ceremonial procession. Meanwhile, on block after block of Chicago's Miracle Mile and at Buckhead Atlanta, plantings as ebullient as any English cottage border urge passersby to get up close and personal with texture and color, even if those encounters transpire through a windshield or over a clutch of shopping bags.

Outside the strict bounds of a public thoroughfare, Hoerr Schaudt often skirts the shortest distance between two points, rolling out serpentine driveways, roundabout paths, and zigzag stairs to suggest the possibility of limitless rambles. Conspiring with gateways and shrubbery in a suspenseful game of hide-and-seek, each twist and bend delays the gratification of discovery. Paving materials and patterns almost subliminally slow or quicken the pace, as well as signal shifts in mood. Stepping-stones and cobbles set entirely different rhythms. Bark and gravel strike a casual tone—for plants and people—that's far removed from the decorum imposed by soigné travertine or solemn granite.

Where energy might flag, the designers spring seductive flora, a tantalizing glimpse of distant scenery, or an extraordinary artifact to rally the spirit of adventure. Journey's end brings a sense of arrival, though the tenor of the welcome varies by destination. "It's all about making places, big or small, that people want to come to and explore," Hoerr adds. "Places that touch them." A secluded woodland pond or bench in an alcove of tall grasses encourages solitary contemplation. The ensemble of a leafy canopy overhead, solid masonry underfoot, and moving water invites congenial get-togethers, from a sit-down on a private terrace to takeout lunches in a civic plaza. Daydreamers peering down from high-rise offices vicariously frequent the alternative city squares of the firm's signature green roofs.

Here and there amid Chicago's vast grid, a diagonal street skews the geometry, retracing some branch of a trail that once led its original inhabitants to the intersection of riverbank and lakeshore. Crossroads between past and present, nature and craft, also recur throughout Hoerr Schaudt's collaborative terrain. While pointing twenty-first-century children to a family beach, a stone staircase looks back to Prairie School pioneers. A campus master plan redirects urban traffic and the evolution of a historic university. At a stadium's underground parking garage, prehistoric geology and innovative engineering converge. Grafting new life onto a botanic garden's stately routes transforms a cultural relic into a must-see civic attraction.

# CHAPTER 1 Path to Plaza

Private Access

Local Traffic

# Garden in the Round

LAKE FOREST, ILLINOIS 1991

Revisiting the very first residential garden he designed in the Chicago area, twenty-five years after laying it out, Doug Hoerr felt that he had come full circle. "There's so much personal history here," he says. "In hindsight, it was kismet." He received the commission shortly after returning from training in England, and the original owners have lovingly cared for the property ever since. Indefatigable champions of public horticulture and open-land preservation, the couple met Hoerr in 1991 through his mentor John Brookes, whose English-style Walled Garden at the Chicago Botanic Garden opened that same year. Hoerr's new clients wryly dismissed any comparison to the walled suburban plot where they had brought up three children over several decades. Their house, a Mediterranean-inspired villa built in 1923, stood close to a major road on a scant acre. Most of the backyard had been given over to play-hardy turf and a smattering of mature trees, symmetrical clipped evergreens, and rectangular dahlia beds.

"Our old garden was quite traditional," the husband remembers. "Nice, though everything was square." "It was really boring," his wife confesses now. "I told Doug we didn't want a single straight line or tiresome formality, and he got that right away."

Hoerr may have banished the T-square from his drawing board, but he did not forsake geometric order. His plan deploys the arc of the draftsman's compass as well as freehand curves to link architecture and vegetation, pond and woodland, light and shade, movement and repose. The entire scheme centers on a circular lawn, a focal point akin to a Jens Jensen council ring in a forest clearing—even if the woodland beyond and the curved, boulder-rimmed pond it embraces are, in fact, naturalistic features of his own devising. "I didn't want the house to ram some hard-edged terrace into the landscape," Hoerr says. "I wanted the landscape to come right up to the house." In that spirit, concave stairs radiate off the lawn and rise, amphitheater style, toward a south-facing, glassed-in loggia where the owners enjoy sitting year-round, looking out.

Plants growing through the steps' gravel treads, a move Hoerr learned from Beth Chatto, bring the garden even closer and merge with gravel walkways that offer a choice of hidden destinations. Even in winter, conifers work to mask outer walls and fences,

**LEFT:** Shallow steps ease the descent from house to lawn. Gravel treads planted with lady's mantle, lamb's ear, thrift, and other perennials merge architecture and garden. **ABOVE RIGHT:** Between arborvitae spires, sarcoxie wintercreeper sheathes the sun porch, composing an evergreen facade. **PREVIOUS PAGES:** Lush rodgersia, hosta, and epimedium catch dappled light between pond and woodland.

visually stretching boundaries to borrow glimpses of neighbors' treetops. An implicit logic governs everything underfoot. Flagstones pave areas that, unlike the gravel surfaces here, are shoveled clear of snow. Gravel's civilized tone seems out of place in the woods, where bark feels more at home, so rather than have different materials run together messily, native stepping-stones mark a neat divide. The wife, an artist who sculpts and paints in her backyard studio, often accompanied Hoerr on trips to Wisconsin quarries to select each weathered rock. Some now provide rustic pedestals for her bronzes, such as the pond-side frog, *Ballet Dreamer*. What could be more *apropos* in a garden that is, to lift a phrase from another discipline, a dance to the music of time?

**LEFT: Mown turf underscores the foliage textures of whitespire birch, Norway spruce, bottlebrush buckeye, and spring-flowering elderberry. ABOVE: Wisconsin stone, a Jens Jensen favorite, paves a side-yard path.**

LEFT: Around the bend where a walk enters the woodland, its surface shifts from "civilized" gravel to "sylvan" bark. Delicate *Iris* 'Caesar's Brother' offsets the pond's weathered-edge boulder outcrop. BELOW: Parallel borders of ostrich fern and hosta, at left, and hardy geranium and pachysandra, at right, curve toward a climactic pair of red Japanese maples.

OPPOSITE, TOP LEFT: One of two wrought-iron posts salvaged from the property's original fence counterbalances a Norway spruce arching over rustic steps. In spring, yellow corydalis lights the way. BOTTOM: Peonies bloom in front of the block-walled studio where one of the owners sculpts and paints. Her husband grows vegetables in raised beds, at right, close to the kitchen door.

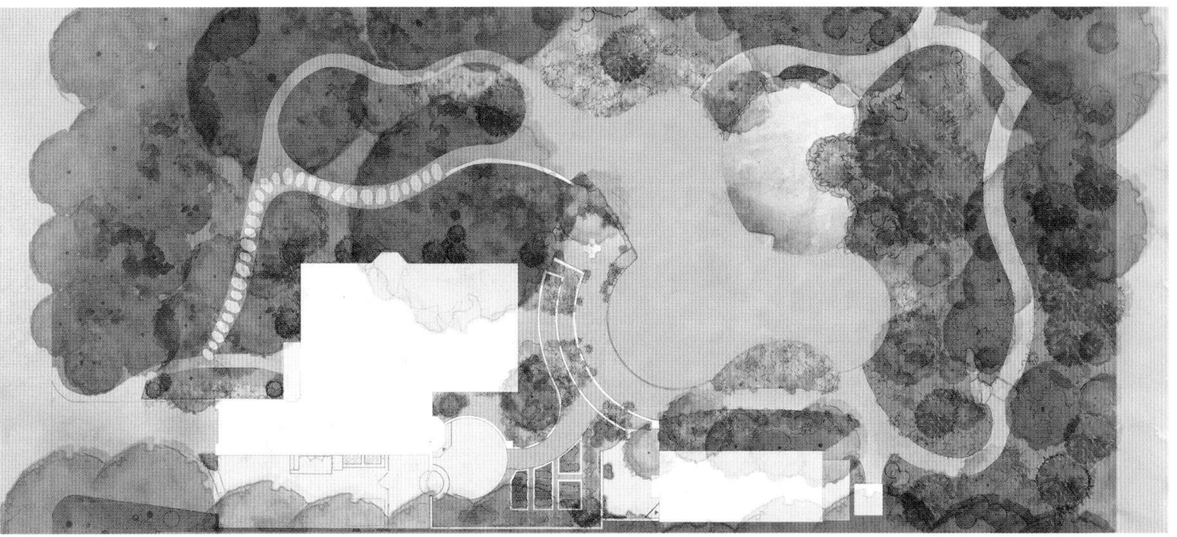

# Renker Residence

INDIAN WELLS, CALIFORNIA 2007



Every stroll through Stacey and Greg Renker's three-quarters of an acre in a country-club community near Palm Springs has been routed as meticulously as a round of golf on the eighteen-hole course next door. In sharp contrast, Doug Hoerr's introductory tour of the property felt like searching through the rough for a lost ball.

Two decades had elapsed since Michael Taylor, California's grand master of late-twentieth-century interior design, redid both the house and garden for prior owners. Hoerr spotted signature Taylor moves—clean lines, luminous white surfaces, indoor/outdoor fluidity—in the sweep of white travertine that crossed floors inside the strongly horizontal house, through glass doors onto the adjacent terrace, and around the swimming pool and spa. Overgrown plantings had smudged the 1980s landscape's crisp edges, blurring boundaries between gregarious and intimate spaces and obscuring wonderful views of the starkly majestic Santa Rosa Mountains.

The Renkers were eager to preserve Taylor's legacy while layering interiors with the richer palette of the Impressionist and postwar contemporary art they collect. With their blessing, Hoerr took a

**RIGHT:** Sequestered between grapefruit trees and sago palms, the travertine path from the entry gate gives no hint of the dramatic reveal at the far end of the right-hand wall. **OPPOSITE:** The path angles to disclose a mountain panorama beyond sentinel fan palms.

similar tack in the garden. He offset the dazzle of the travertine with radiant greenery and incandescent bloom, sometimes even matching the hues of leaves and petals to pictures hung in a room that overlooks them. Inventive extrapolation from Taylor's geometry signals a domestic hierarchy for pathways as well as destinations. Rectangular expanses of continuous travertine paving mark areas shared by family and guests, such as the formal dining terrace where the Renkers usually entertain. Individual stepping-stones staggered through mown turf denote more casual zones, such as the spa, separate courtyards off the master suite and the three sons' bedrooms, and a shortcut to the golf course.

When Hoerr initially briefed his clients on the rhythmic patterns and color harmonies he had in mind, Greg Renker says, "It was like hearing Pat Metheny play for the first time." For visitors to the completed landscape, discoveries begin inside the front gate. There, a travertine-carpeted dogleg slows

**OPPOSITE: The same stone used for paving in front unites the rear pool and steps with the white-painted brick house. COUNTERCLOCKWISE, FROM BELOW: Brilliant *Argyranthemum* 'Butterfly,' delphinium, and Indian hawthorn crown a cascade. Succulents fill a basket-weave pot. The fire trough warms cool desert evenings.**

footsteps to a ceremonial pace; high walls, a citrus allée, a sculptural bench, and stone antiquities point the way and whet anticipation. Hoerr saved his climactic revelation for the far side of the residence, where he removed an intrusive garden parapet to insert a gracious axial stairway. This bold stroke opened a dramatic through-line linking the pool, terrace, house, and front walk. Two stone Buddhas face each other from the opposite ends of this enfilade, reminding all who pass through to reflect on the peace that surrounds them.

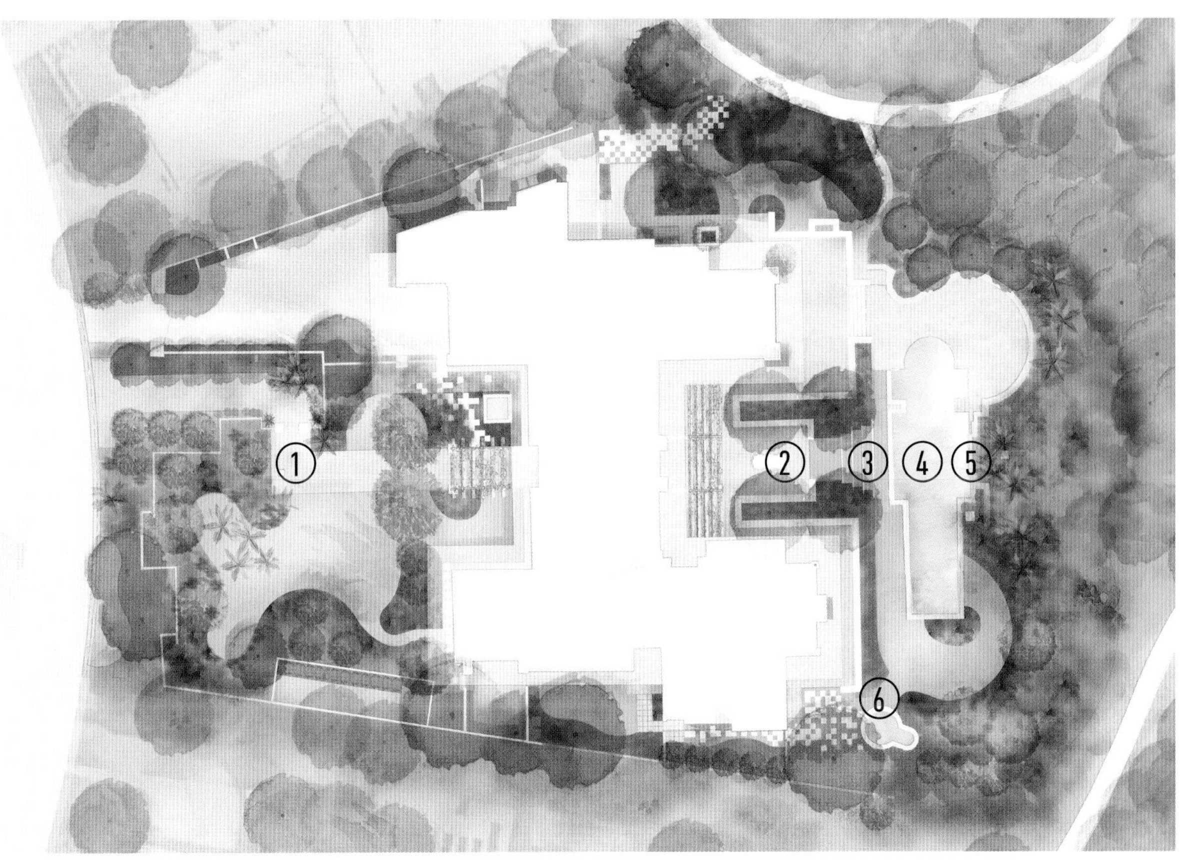


LEFT: Sinewy African sumac trees (*Rhus lancea*) and cloud-pruned Japanese mock-orange (*Pittosporum tobira* 'Wheeler's Dwarf') soften the formal symmetry of the dining terrace, which centers on a Michael Taylor–designed travertine table. Annuals edging the lawn steps are replaced seasonally to ensure constant color. Glass doors mirror the Buddha gazing back across the pool.

1 Entry Walkway
2 Dining Terrace
3 Stairway
4 Pool
5 Waterfall
6 Spa

LEFT: In a sanctuary outside the master suite, widely spaced stepping-stones encourage contemplative strolls. Pedestals for guardian deities are fringed by *Dietes* and variegated mondo grass. A callery pear tree casts welcome shade while bougainvillea fans out across the sunny far wall.

OPPOSITE, CLOCKWISE FROM TOP LEFT: Staggered pavers veer left at an olive tree, routing private cart access to the golf course next door. Kalanchoe and cyclamen flowers brighten dining-terrace planters and table. Coreopsis gilds the spa. Next to a minimalist travertine fountain at the front door, potted hibiscus shines. Pale yellow roses bloom beside a diminutive lawn. Scarlet kalanchoe and an olive tree's pale trunk call out the diverse foliage patterns of variegated ginger, leopard plant (*Farfugium japonicum*), and flowering maple (*Abutilon* x *hybridum*).

# Lake Michigan Estate

CHICAGO'S NORTH SHORE 2007–2016

 There's no way to reach Lake Michigan without passing through New England at this property near Chicago. The owners, a couple with young children, called upon Robert A.M. Stern Architects to design their house in a relaxed Georgian style reminiscent of farmsteads they had admired in the East. Bringing Yankee understatement to the complexities of a modern program and Midwestern terrain tested the navigational skills of Doug Hoerr and Stern partner Randy Correll. Their assignment called for downplaying the visual impact of the 16,000-square-foot residence on its three-acre site, ensuring privacy from a busy suburban street in front and neighbors to either side, maximizing outdoor space for family recreation, preserving a stand of centenarian oak trees atop a waterfront bluff, and linking that high ground to a new boathouse and beach below.

By design, the main house rambles to skirt the oaks. Its varied massing and materials suggest an old structure that has grown in stages, prizing comfort over show. "Like our clients, Doug and I wanted the building to be revealed in parts," Correll says. "Both of us got obsessed with tying the house into the history we created for it." The landscape narrative begins with a gated stone boundary wall opening onto a drive whose curves Hoerr craftily plotted to afford only discreet glimpses of a cottage-like gable peeking through greenery. Upon arrival at the front porch, a measure of formality unfolds through a network of paths and garden rooms dovetailed into the architecture and framed by low walls of the same Connecticut fieldstone used on several facades. Paving weaves mellow carpets of reclaimed brick, bluestone, and granite that imply the gradual accretion of a country house's legacy. Terraces and lawns sweep across the bluff with genteel ease. Their mannerly repose only heightens a thrilling surprise tucked just beyond the edge: rough-hewn Wisconsin limestone steps marching downhill toward the shore. Hoerr's staircase—which practically incorporates the fragments of a Prairie School forerunner—surveys an inland seascape where the East Coast seems but a distant memory.

ABOVE: On the far side of the property, atop a bluff overlooking the lake, Hoerr linked outdoor living areas with a continuous stone "podium." The bluestone pool deck rests on stainless-steel grade beams that invisibly lift it above the vulnerable roots of ancient oaks. OPPOSITE: A model of discretion alongside a public road, Doug Hoerr's recessed entrance gateway opens onto a winding drive lined with trees and shrubs that carefully screen the house designed by Robert A.M. Stern Architects.

ABOVE: Playing off Stern's Georgian idiom—complete with Connecticut fieldstone facades—gardens near the house reinterpret Colonial Revival forerunners. Boxwood and brick mingle comfortably with catmint, lady's mantle, iris, delphinium, phlox, astilbe, and other classics. A Japanese maple (*Acer palmatum* 'Viridis') and two whitespire birches rise to architectural scale. OPPOSITE, CLOCKWISE FROM TOP LEFT: In one of his own fieldstone walls, Hoerr installed a dummy gate to imply that a path continues into what is, in fact, a neighbor's yard. Just as the varied materials of the house suggest a history of expansion, the patchwork of reclaimed brick from Skokie, Illinois, and paving stone from New England in a zigzag path gives the patina of age. A clipped-box parterre outside the wife's office comports with her symmetrical doorway while an off-center star magnolia relieves strict formality. *Iris ensata* 'Snowflake,' water lettuce, and water hyacinth inhabit a traditional wall fountain.

OPPOSITE: Hoerr extrapolated his shoreline stairway from remnants of one on the site, reputedly the work of Prairie School designer Alfred Caldwell. Wisconsin limestone similar to that in the estate's reconstructed roadside wall erects a suitably rugged base for naturalistic drifts of juniper and bayberry among the bur and white oaks looming above.

THIS PAGE, COUNTERCLOCKWISE FROM LEFT: Farther downhill, masonry pockets harbor Bonica shrub roses, sedums, and hostas for close-up enjoyment. The geometric ensemble of lawn steps, pool terrace, and pool house atop the bluff presents a sharp contrast to the free-form tumble downhill. Before touching bottom, the stairway lands on the roof deck of a new boathouse; Hoerr hid the majority of its bulk by recontouring the slope. Drought-tolerant dune grasses transition the property to the restored beach and a new groin that stabilizes its sandy shore.

Crate&Barrel
SUMMERHOUSE
TO
90
94
SPEED LIMIT
30
CITY INFORMATION

# Crate & Barrel Store

CHICAGO 1991–PRESENT

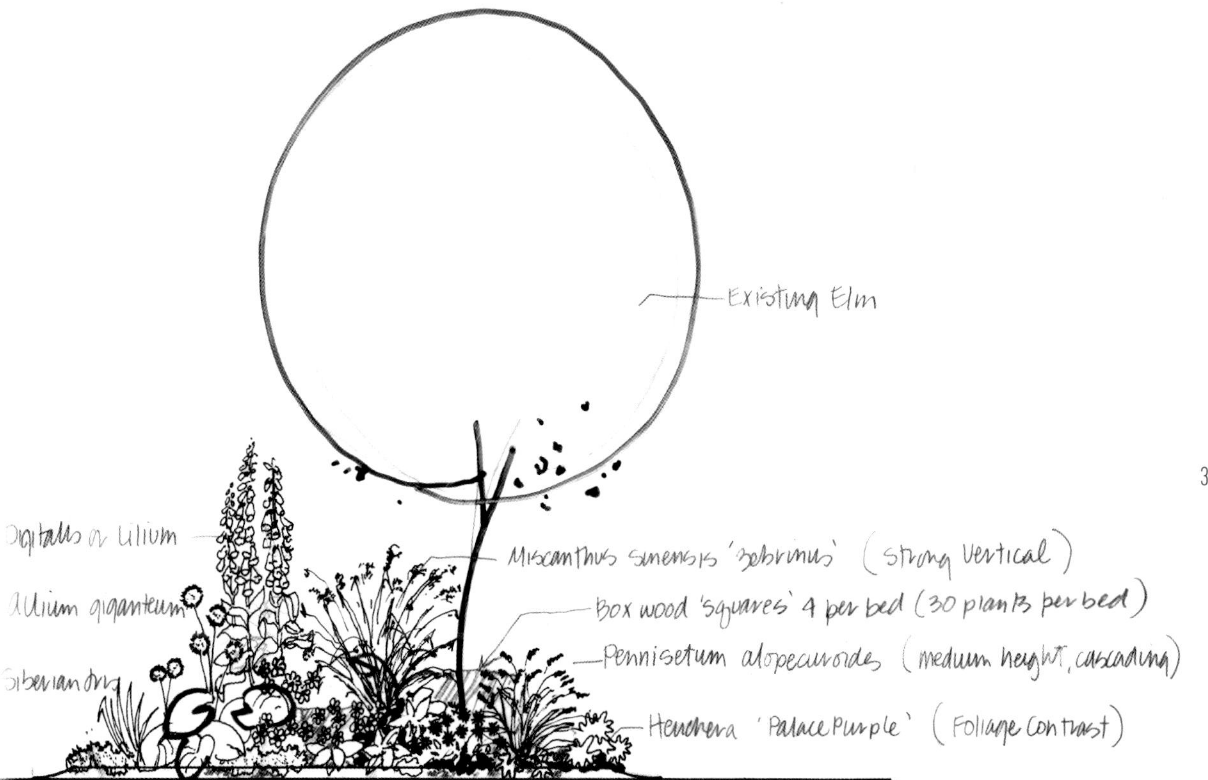




Missed opportunities stared Doug Hoerr in the face as he walked up to Crate & Barrel's flagship store on North Michigan Avenue in Chicago during the summer of 1991. He had been hired simply to install lighting for four sidewalk planting beds identical to those that fronted other upscale stores along what Chicagoans called the Magnificent Mile. "I'd landed there soon after leaving England," Hoerr says, "and it was hard for me to understand what was magnificent about that street." The monotonous landscaping—a lanky elm tree at the center of each bed rimmed by a patch of lawn and a low fence—stood in bland contrast to the stylish, colorful home furnishings visible through the store's glass facade.

The company's founders, Carole and Gordon Segal, had based their retail success on innovative design, consistent value, and strategic risk-taking. Hoerr readily convinced them that it would take a lot more than outdoor lights to create a sidewalk as distinctive, engaging, and contemporary as their sales floors. "I pitched gardens as hip and accessible as the lifestyle they marketed," Hoerr says. "Dynamic, complex gardens. Not the typical landscaper's spring and summer 'bedding-out' you saw back then—uniform rows of salvias, marigolds, geraniums, or other run-of-the-mill annuals."

Hoerr nimbly adapted the flourishes of English borders, softened by a gentle climate, to the bottom line of Midwestern curb appeal and weather. In his presentation sketches for the 8-by-14-foot beds, as in the streetwise plantings that realized them, the designer combined an ambitious range of annuals, perennials, bulbs, and ornamental grasses into a four-season rotation of contrasting textures, shapes, and sizes. Canny scheduling ensured that when individual varieties faded, fresh replacements would step in to maintain the flamboyant effect. Total makeovers heralded succeeding waves of seasonal merchandise or coordinated with a prophetic colorway for china or upholstery: "If Marimekko fabrics made a comeback in their windows, we'd have a Marimekko palette in the beds outside." Once the Segals bought into Hoerr's concept, his eye-catching displays became a Crate & Barrel trademark. The retailer went on to order site-specific gardens for two dozen stores nationwide.

From opening day on Michigan Avenue, people gathered around the three sidewalk planting beds as spontaneously as they might hang out in a pocket park. The fences came into demand as short-term benches. Pedestrians who hurried past neighboring shops would suddenly stop to take in the latest floral décor. Reports that this garden buzz had boosted in-store traffic at Crate & Barrel prompted nearby Michigan Avenue merchants, including Burberry, to commission their own parkway plots from Hoerr. The designer, though, had no inkling of bigger plans underway, which would soon steer him off the curb and into the fast lane.

**OPPOSITE:** By transforming city sidewalks into garden paths, storefront beds encourage pedestrians to pause and window shop, especially when plantings change seasonally to complement merchandise. This tropical-looking summer display mixes bromeliads, philodendrons, Japanese forest grass, and coleus. **ABOVE:** In a presentation sketch, a tree, shrubs, and perennials create a year-round armature for transitory bulbs and annuals.

THIS PAGE, CLOCKWISE FROM ABOVE: The original turfed beds did little to relieve a bleak stretch of pavement. An early plan outlines robust contrasts of texture and shape. Obligatory fall chrysanthemums take an offbeat turn around the tree with bird-of-paradise, kale, and sedge. OPPOSITE, CLOCKWISE FROM BELOW: For a different year's autumn décor, mums partner with pansies, ornamental cabbage, and foxtail ferns alongside evergreen boxwood and the fading foliage of maiden grass and Japanese maples. A Marimekko floral fabric was planned to provide a backdrop to Crate & Barrel window displays one spring, so the fall before, Doug Hoerr planted tulip bulbs outdoors to coincide exactly—in bloom time and palette—with the view behind plate glass.

# Michigan Avenue

CHICAGO 1991–2016

The plants had hardly taken root outside Crate & Barrel before Chicago's environmentalist mayor, Richard M. Daley, took note. In short order he named Gordon Segal and Doug Hoerr to a planning committee for the "greening" of Michigan Avenue through a creative amalgam of public and private funds. "At that point," Hoerr says, "the only color on the roadway came from yellow stripes down the middle." In 1992 construction began on a thirty-three-block line of concrete median planters: a scenic upgrade for North Michigan Avenue's affluent Miracle Mile, as well as a green light for renewal of the avenue's less prosperous blocks south of the Chicago River.

Hoerr framed much of his landscape design as "beautification through the windshield." While he and architect John Buenz analyzed the ideal median height for enjoyment by passing motorists as well as pedestrians (twenty-one inches, they concluded), Hoerr was sizing up the aesthetic obstacles that everything planted there would confront. "My goal was to make the horticulture so bold that it looked ready to jump out of the planters and compete with any skyscraper," he explains. Hence his audacious leaps with flamboyant foliage, towering stalks, and hot-colored flowers. "Back then, cool Sissinghurst tones—lavender, silver, white—were the rage, but here they would have melted into the grays of asphalt, concrete, and steel." And, he decided, the fifty-seven median planters must outpace their kinetic environs with turn-on-a-dime seasonal rotations. "We couldn't tell business owners and city officials who were footing the bill, 'Be patient . . .' Everything had to look good from day one."

The impact of each horticultural tour de force relies on knowing which plants will withstand exhaust and other pollution, which will thrive in specific urban microclimates, which will show up on schedule. A choice of species or cultivar may hinge on measuring the exact angle at which high-rise windows bounce the sunlight onto a shady median. It may mean gauging how the warmth from an underground parking garage will accelerate spring bloom, or anticipating how gusts off the lake blow through an intersection. Planting usually occurs after evening rush hours, to minimize interference from moving vehicles and persistent kibitzers.

Initially, even the acquisition of suitable plant varieties demanded logistical derring-do. "Castor beans and sweet potato vine were novelties in Chicago then, and people here didn't know any cool-season plants besides mums. Our first fall, I had to go to five different growers in search of ornamental kale, cabbage, and violas." On average, some 24,500 individual plants are required to create the billowing exuberance of a single summer or autumn display. It takes 110,000 tulip bulbs to produce the spring awakening—after a winter nap under protective sod and evergreen boughs—that has now become part of the civic calendar.

Grateful commuters, shoppers, and cabbies sent thank-you notes and paintings of the gardens

**RIGHT: High-powered horticulture holds its own against tall buildings in this motorist's-eye view of the Miracle Mile. Trailing nasturtiums and petunias flash bright colors while hydrangeas and papyrus dominate their own midblock skyline. LEFT: The north-south spine of median islands provides 27,000 square feet of beds for successive spring, summer, and fall plantings.**

THE MAGNIFICENT MILE
BUS STOP
TOW ZONE

to Hoerr Schaudt's office. Local and national media lauded the central role of horticulture in what soon became a model for other cities. "Mayor Daley, of course, loved it," Hoerr recalls. "Then every alderman said, 'I want that for my ward.'" By the twentieth anniversary of the Michigan Avenue planters' début, the firm calculates that ninety-eight total miles of medians had blossomed on Chicago streets.

ABOVE LEFT: Tedium ruled the road before planters marched down the avenue in 1993. ABOVE RIGHT: The following year's inaugural tulip parade has since become a popular rite of spring, as has the annual public giveaway of discarded bulbs. RIGHT: Spring's early monocrop yields to the diversity of combos like *Heliopsis* 'Summer Sun' with butterfly weed, sweet potato vine, *Plectranthus* 'Silver Shield,' castor bean, and *Cordyline* 'Baueri.'

DERBY
8.9.12
ADOPT
A DUCK
WGN Radio 720am

ABOVE: An average “layout week” for seasonal planting involves three contractors, representatives from the City of Chicago and local businesses, twenty Hoerr Schaudt designers, and a thirty-five-person volunteer installation crew from the Christian Industrial League that starts work after the evening rush hour. LEFT: Street trees’ hazy fall foliage sets off concrete cornucopias brimming with robust cabbage (*Brassica oleracea* ‘Ruby Perfection’), chrysanthemums, and fountain grass (*Pennisetum* ‘Princess Caroline’).

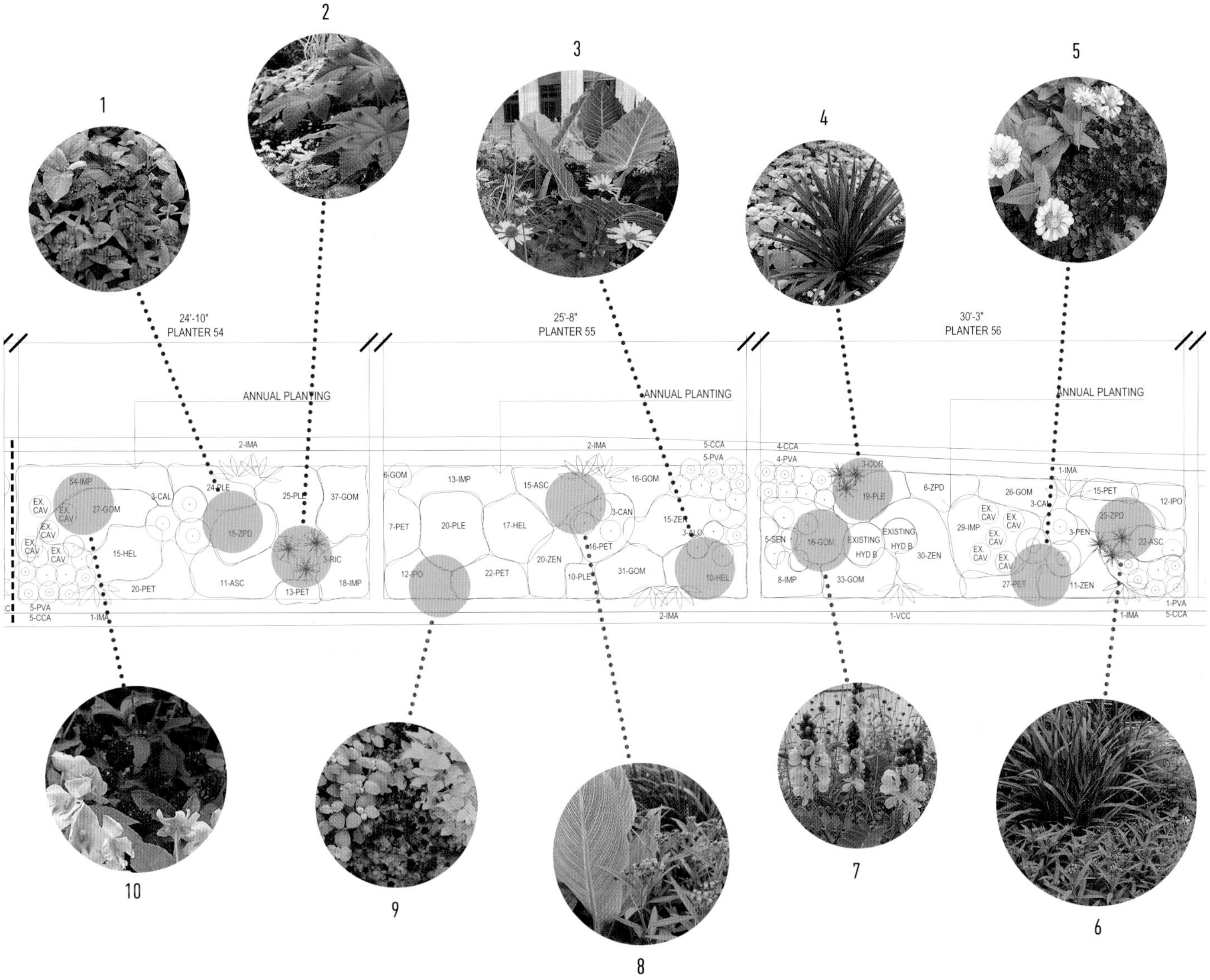

## PLANTING PLAN
## MEDIANS 54, 55, 56, 57

24'-10" PLANTER 54

25'-8" PLANTER 55

30'-3" PLANTER 56

ANNUAL PLANTING

1. *Zinnia* 'Profusion Double Fire,' silver spurflower (*Plectranthus argentatus* 'Silver Shield')
2. Castor bean (*Ricinus communis*)
3. False sunflower (*Heliopsis* 'Summer Sun'), elephant ear (*Alocasia macrorrhiza* 'Lutea')
4. *Cordyline* 'Baueri'
5. *Zinnia* 'Envy,' *Petunia* 'Blue Wave'
6. Purple fountain grass (*Pennisetum purpureum* 'Princess'), tropical milkweed (*Asclepias curassavica*)
7. Popcorn senna (*Senna alata*)
8. *Canna* 'Pretoria', tropical milkweed (*Asclepias curassavica*)
9. Silver spurflower (*Plectranthus argentatus* 'Silver Shield'), *Petunia* 'Blue Wave,' sweet potato vine (*Ipomoea batatas* 'Marguerita')
10. Globe amaranth *(Gomphrena globosa* 'QIS Purple'), *Impatiens* 'Fusion Glow'

ABOVE: Diagrams for three of Michigan Avenue's fifty-seven median planters illustrate the paint-by-numbers exactitude of each layout. Combinations must be keyed to sun and wind exposure, shadows cast by buildings, and other conditions that can vary from one block to the next. BELOW: Each season thoroughly alters the containerized landscapes. Not shown is their habitual winter blanket of turf and evergreen boughs that protect spring's tulip bulbs.

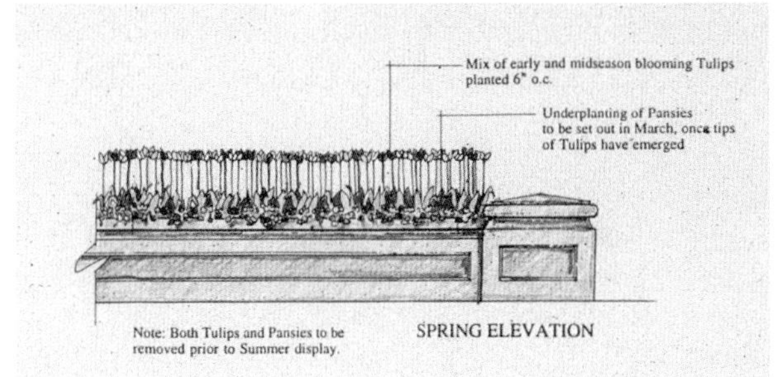


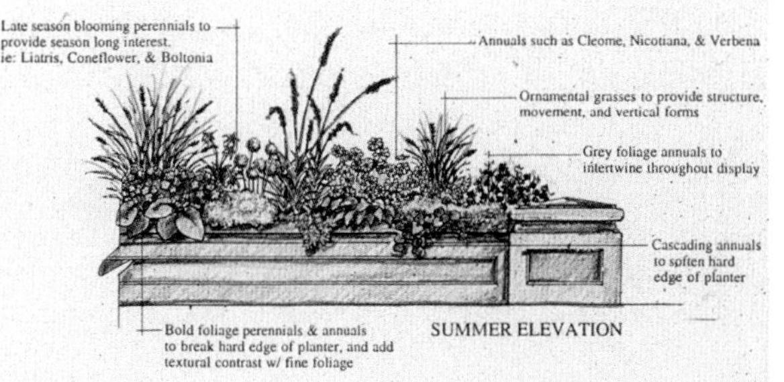


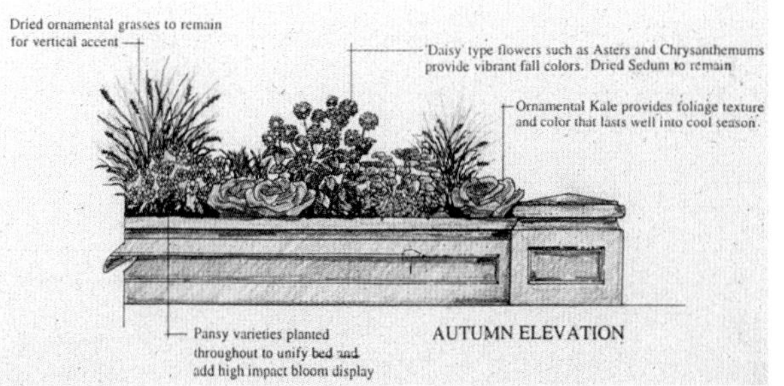

# Daley Plaza

RICHARD J. DALEY CENTER, CHICAGO 1996



Peter Schaudt wasn't imagining Renaissance arcades or marble saints when he dubbed this modernist square "the Italian piazza of Chicago." One of the city's liveliest, best-loved urban spaces, the plaza has always adjoined its high-rise municipal building, the Richard J. Daley Center, designed by Jacques Brownson and completed in 1965. The wide-open courtyard honored the tower's Miesian reticence with a granite-paved expanse, a half-block area tersely punctuated by three lone honey locust trees in separate planters. Two years later, the unveiling of a fifty-foot-tall Picasso sculpture on the plaza clinched its iconic status.

While three decades in the open air bestowed a coveted patina on the tower's Cor-Ten steel frame, constant wear and tear had scarred its granite surround with hazardous, unsightly cracks. Schaudt plotted a thorough-yet-inconspicuous rejuvenation overseen by a watchful Mayor Richard M. Daley, son of the Civic Center's namesake. "It felt like plastic surgery," he said. The program set three main goals: replace the thin stone pavers with more durable lookalikes, double the tree count without changing the number or location of planters, and leave the plaza's landmark character intact.

Smart sleuthing led the project team to Illinois University's Chicago campus, where demolition had begun on unfashionable 1960s Brutalist walkways built with massive hunks of the same granite specified for the contemporary Civic Center plaza. Hand in hand with his engineer and contractor, Schaudt said, "We sliced granite like pastrami into pavers significantly thicker than the old ones. All that expensive stone was ours for the cost of hauling it away from IUC." Adding greenery posed different

LEFT: Prior to renovation, hazardous cracked granite pavers and meager vegetation detracted from the Civic Center's landmark tower and Picasso sculpture. ABOVE: The picturesque grove of honey locusts now fringing Chicago City Hall, on the plaza's western edge, looks as if its roots reach deep into native soil. In fact, thanks to deftly camouflaged engineering, the trees grow inside the walled confines of pits sunken into a lower concourse.

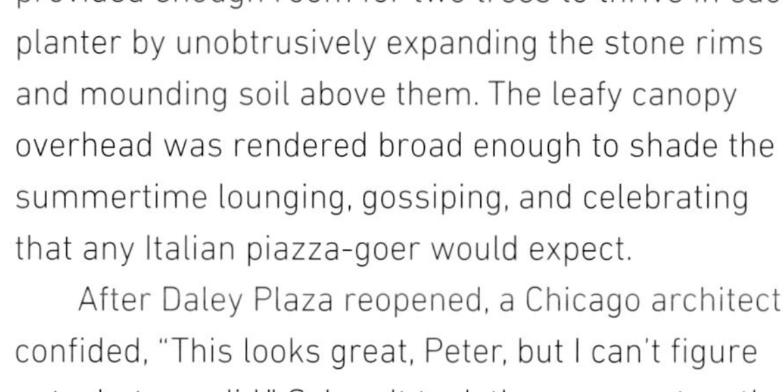



challenges. The new sextet of thirty-five-foot-tall honey locusts had substantial eleven-foot root balls—truckers had to deflate their tires to squeeze their cargo under the L girders—and the original Civic Center tree pits, boxed in by plaza substructure, were too cramped for healthy root spread. Schaudt provided enough room for two trees to thrive in each planter by unobtrusively expanding the stone rims and mounding soil above them. The leafy canopy overhead was rendered broad enough to shade the summertime lounging, gossiping, and celebrating that any Italian piazza-goer would expect.

After Daley Plaza reopened, a Chicago architect confided, "This looks great, Peter, but I can't figure out what you did." Schaudt took the comment as the highest compliment to his craft.

CLOCKWISE FROM TOP: A cross-section of the plaza shows soil mounded above root balls to permit multiple plantings in pits originally intended for single trees. A crane lowers a full-grown tree into one of the pits. Elsewhere, new raised granite planters with broad ledges double as seating for plaza visitors and security barriers along an adjacent street.

# Apple Stores

CHICAGO 2003 and 2010

This tale of upward mobility began when Apple Computer Inc. engaged Doug Hoerr to devise sidewalk plantings for the company's first stand-alone Chicago store, then under construction on North Michigan Avenue. The crisp geometry of Hoerr's scheme—a symmetrical pair of elms rising from rectanglar planters—complemented the suave minimalism of the building, by architects Bohlin Cywinski Jackson. Meanwhile, though, the landscape designer had fixed his gaze on a higher plane—the flat gray roof around a skylight overlooked by Apple's fourth-story penthouse meeting room. As the recently appointed chairman of Mayor Daley's Green Roof Committee, whose only local exemplar so far was a green roof on City Hall, Hoerr saw his main chance for a breakthrough into private-sector commissions: an installation for the Miracle Mile's hottest new retailer.

The architects enthusiastically welcomed his idea; Apple's on-site representatives were skeptical. Then, a few days later, Hoerr recalls, "A guy phoned me and said, 'Steve Jobs wants you to explain this to him. Come to Cupertino on Friday for an eight a.m." He did. "In walks Jobs in his turtleneck and torn jeans." Hoerr stated the environmental case for a living roof that would temper the urban heat-island effect, reduce harmful stormwater runoff, and lower energy consumption. "Finally I asked, 'If someone like you doesn't lead by example, Steve, who will?' After a pause he said, 'Okay. I'll do it.' One of his entourage pulled me aside later and said, 'Be careful, or next you'll be doing his house.'"

Back on North Michigan, it took a mere twelve hours to install the 2,400-square-foot carpet of drought-tolerant succulents, *Sedum floriferum* 'Weihenstephaner Gold', *S. hybridum*, and *S. kamtschaticum*, graphically bordered by black La Paz pebble laid in the gutters. With normal precipitation, the sedum needs watering only three or four times a year, and dense planting discourages weeds. The flagship store's well-publicized opening gained extra kudos when observers in neighboring hotel, office, and retail towers discovered that they too could visually access the greenery.

In 2009, when Apple Inc. retained Hoerr Schaudt to partner with Bohlin Cywinski Jackson on a second flagship store, in Chicago's up-and-coming Lincoln Park neighborhood, the client specified both ground-level and rooftop landscapes. The architectural footprint on this busy triangular site, which also included a subway station entrance and a café, left ample room for an open-air plaza. "Apple agreed with us that this should be a gathering place for people, whether or not they were likely customers," Peter Schaudt said. "That meant trees and flowers, portable furniture, water features shallow enough to work in this climate." From the rooftop sedum to the stone planters down below, every square inch required inspection by a design squad Steve Jobs air-lifted in from California. Full-size plywood mockups of the planters had to pass muster before the granite could be quarried in China and hand-finished in Italy. Shaudt remarked, "We could have been detailing packaging for the next iPhone launch."

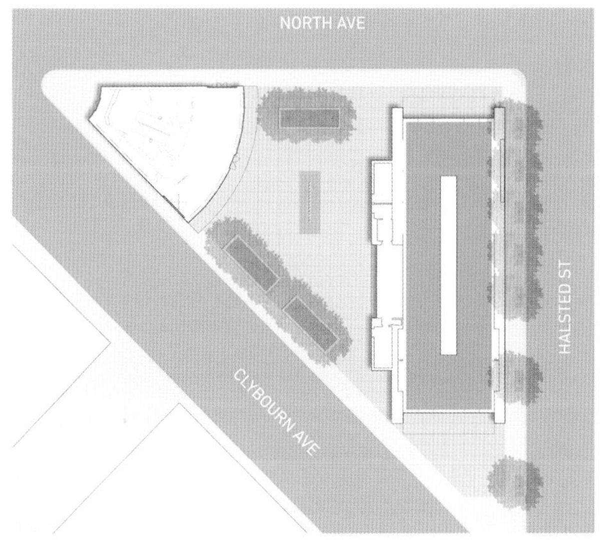

OPPOSITE, FROM TOP: At the North Michigan Avenue location, beds edged in honed sandstone extend the Apple aesthetic outside, while the American elm matches similar trees up and down the street. A meeting-room window faces the green roof and overlooks the sedum that borders the skylight. THIS PAGE, CLOCKWISE FROM ABOVE: The Lincoln Park plaza is wedged between the store and a subway entrance. Granite planters add public seating. Stainless steel rims this store's green roof.

ETRO

# Buckhead Atlanta

ATLANTA, GEORGIA 2014

In a city where upscale pedestrian shopping districts are rare, lavishly planted sidewalks set Buckhead Atlanta apart. OPPOSITE: This ensemble makes a statement by coordinating bold elephant ear and *Canna* 'Bengal Tiger' with chic 'Velvet Mocha' coleus, 'Limelight' hydrangea, and *Asclepias tuberosa*. ABOVE: More than 33,000 plants establish street-level intimacy amid the eight-acre complex of stores, restaurants, apartments, and offices.

Stilettos are sensible shoes for a garden stroll. Just ask any fashionista in Buckhead Atlanta, the luxurious enclave of specialty stores, restaurants, apartments, and offices where stopping to smell the flowers is as au courant as trying on Jimmy Choos or sipping an Aperol spritz.

This area once marked the center of a rural village that later swelled into Atlanta's posh Buckhead district, aka "the Beverly Hills of the South." In 2011, when San Diego–based developer OliverMcMillan purchased eight largely vacant acres—bulldozed by a previous entrepreneur—for the construction of a $600 million mixed-use project called Buckhead Atlanta, onlookers anticipated a mall dressed up as a Southern Rodeo Drive.

Rather than strive for aloof glamour, however, McMillan's plan evoked the familiar grid of an "urban village" in hopes of reweaving the new complex into greater Buckhead. More radical for car-centric Atlanta—and a site one block away from the hectic Peachtree Road corridor—was the imaginative landscaping of sidewalks and plazas to buffer pedestrians from motor traffic and tempt them to linger. Hoerr Schaudt retained city-mandated sidewalk widths but replaced standard pavement in the "amenity zones" that edge the roadways with sumptuous parkway plantings anchored by mature trees. "Their stature gives the air of an established neighborhood our client wanted," Doug Hoerr says. "There's also the instant gratification that retailers and restaurateurs insist on—plus shade from the Georgia sun."

Hoerr Schaudt's design team convinced the city to approve tree trunks at least twice the 3-inch-caliper thickness stipulated by municipal ordinance. The 140 specimens include forty-foot-tall oaks with twenty-five-foot-wide canopies, which had to be lifted over buildings by crane and positioned via two-way radio. A sand-based structural soil, which the designers installed under all sidewalks, tolerates compaction while maintaining the aeration that roots need to survive. Consistent pruning of lower branches ensures tenants' signs and show windows remain unobstructed to drivers and pedestrians.

More than ten species of shrubs and perennials, as well as forty-one varieties of annuals, thrive in the curbside gardens and other three-season plantings. To enhance Buckhead Atlanta's subtle architectural diversity—conceived by Gensler, Pappageorge Haymes Partners, and Smallwood, Reynolds, Stewart, Stewart—which implies evolution over time, Hoerr Schaudt developed a compatible trio of horticultural styles. Project manager Michael Skowlund sums up these genres as Classic Southern Garden style: "Low boxwood hedges framing old favorites like iris, roses, and cosmos in white and pastels"; Michigan Avenue, "Abundant layers of bright annuals like you-know-where in Chicago"; and "Bold and graphic, geometric blocks of perennials and shrubs accented with flowering annuals."

The team's brief for walkable streetscapes encompassed every detail of paving design. "Our mantra here was 'inch by inch,'" Hoerr says.

Cobblestone-like roadway pavers allude to Buckhead past. The curbs and planter rims are ruggedly handsome Georgia granite. Sidewalks juxtapose more granite with dark, fine-grained basalt and smooth, integrally colored concrete for urbane contrast and variety. With a second phase of construction due to break ground in late 2017, Buckhead's well-heeled present marches on.

Containers vary in shape and scale, as do the plants they hold, to differentiate individual enclaves within this village built from scratch. ABOVE: In tall, tapered pots, curly willow branches rise from cushions of blue Senetti. ABOVE RIGHT: Georgia granite curbing showcases a floral palette keyed to fall fashion. Annuals like these début—and exit—on a three-season schedule of rotations. RIGHT: In one of many nooks designed for leisurely enjoyment, wallflowers and spring tulips bloom beneath a bountiful urn.

ABOVE LEFT: More mature trees, such as these oaks, instantly lend new construction an air of established maturity and provide welcome shade. All trees were purchased, root-pruned, and limbed up two years prior to installation. ABOVE RIGHT: Regular pruning keeps storefront signage in clear view of passing vehicles. RIGHT: Along with dense underplantings, sturdy trunks reassuringly separate foot traffic from roadways.

# North Park University

CHICAGO, 1997–PRESENT

One lingering problem clouded North Park College's confident advance to university status in 1991: a campus that didn't make the grade. Crisscrossed by city streets and lacking the image of intellectual distinction established by a central quad or a cohesive architectural style, the thirty-acre site disoriented freshmen more than welcomed them to academe. "You could have driven right through without realizing this was even a campus, let alone a historic one," Doug Hoerr recalls.

Indeed, North Park traces its roots to 1891, when the Swedish Covenant Church erected a theological seminary, today's Old Main, on rural marshland along the North Branch of the Chicago River. A century's worth of ad hoc expansions and urban sprawl produced the muddle that Hoerr was asked to sort out in the ten-acre area comprising Old Main and other landmarks, classroom facilities for undergraduate liberal arts courses, and the present seminary, Nyvall Hall. Shoehorned between them he found inadequate outdoor spaces for student recreation, worn-out plantings, and haphazard paths and service roads. Plans to raze the obsolete library and administration building while constructing a new library elsewhere confronted Hoerr with a dilemma: "At last, North Park could have the open space it needed, but its academic and spiritual heart—the new library and Nyvall Hall—would still be cut off from the rest of campus by a city street and alley clogged with parked cars, power lines, and, too often, mountains of plowed snow."

By closing off the street and alley to through traffic and burying the power lines (in conjunction with architect Bill Ketcham of VOA Associates), Hoerr erased physical and visual barriers to cross-campus circulation. This left him free to delineate pleasant gathering places and walkways that reinforce the patterns of North Park life, both communal and personal—an ongoing mission for Carl E. Balsam, the university's executive vice president, CFO, and manager of campus development. In Hoerr's scheme, a grand diagonal marks the shortest distance between Old Main and the library, while curved "nodes" at major intersections feature low seating walls designed for collegial pauses. A secular addendum to Biblical texts inscribed on some of the masonry capstones might as well be E. M. Forster's "Only connect," because strengthening vital bonds is the leitmotif of the North Park master plan.

The cohorts of ornamental grasses that have extensively revised pathways throughout North Park also punctuate destinations for every sort of campus activity. OPPOSITE: A thicket of *Miscanthus sinensis* 'Morning Light' loosely defines a study alcove. TOP RIGHT: The Georgian Revival entrance gate outside Old Main, which Hoerr Schaudt designed to harmonize with various historic buildings here, also affirms the university's presence within its diverse neighborhood on Chicago's Northwest Side. RIGHT: Architectural brickwork is echoed by borders of hard-wearing, cost-effective asphalt walks. Major intersections, such as this one near Brandel Library, are paved with brick. Symmetrical swaths of *Panicum virgatum* 'Shenandoah' encircle it.

EMERGENCY

Hoerr's most gregarious landscape is the broad campus green that transformed the former library site. This relaxed "quad" hosts everything from intramural ballgames and fencing practice to study dates and sunbaths. Disparate buildings are linked by pathways consistently paved in asphalt edged with red brick, for "a warm, historic feel that isn't tied to a specific style." It is horticultural fellowship, though, that most memorably embraces daily comings and goings. In addition to planting hundreds of trees and shrubs for structure, Hoerr introduced multitudes of native and ornamental grasses selected for their ability to hold up under the weight of heavy snow. An all-season chorus, they wave toward halls of learning and welcome residents of neighboring blocks. They murmur around intimate retreats for solitary reading and earnest conversation. They stand witness to every rite of passage on what is now, indeed, a campus.

OPPOSITE: Along this approach to North Park Theological Seminary, stone copings of low curved walls are incised with Scriptural quotations. Pinkish tufts of *Calamagrostis* x *acutiflora* 'Karl Foerster' rise behind *Hydrangea arborescens* (left) and 'Knockout' roses edged with lady's mantle. All plants were chosen for low-maintenance care. RIGHT: The bricks paving this "node" radiate from a stone roundel bearing the university seal. Low walls promote outdoor get-togethers.

The landscape honors every phase of the academic year. THIS PAGE, CLOCKWISE FROM TOP: Sugar maples turn gold in early fall. Spring's daffodils and grape hyacinths flower among ornamental grasses sheared for new growth to sprout. In all four seasons, linden trees accentuate the symmetry of a grassy oval. Late-blooming *Hydrangea paniculata* 'Tardiva' is a fall-semester standout. Frost illuminates the winter pallor of *Miscanthus sinensis* 'Morning Light.' OPPOSITE: A chorus of summer greens ranges from 'Gro-Low' sumac to midrange maiden grass to oak and honey-locust leaves on high.

# Dwarf Conifer Garden

CHICAGO BOTANIC GARDEN, GLENCOE, ILLINOIS 2008

Since opening in 1988, this has remained one of the foremost collections of small cone-bearing shrubs and trees in North America, an invaluable resource for botanists and home gardeners alike. But its only entrance—a steep, narrow path disappearing uphill behind a dense allée of clipped lindens—seemed discreet to the point of invisibility. Much of the public walked right by.

The wakeup call came in 2007 with the CBG's decision to have Doug Hoerr renovate the display garden for its twentieth anniversary. Thanks to his apprenticeship with Adrian Bloom, both a dwarf conifer breeder and a designer, Hoerr grasped the biological diversity of these plants, as well as their aesthetic and environmental potential. "In a world with less and less water," he explains, "people should know how tough many dwarf conifers are. Many grow naturally on the arid edges of mountains and screes, which is why we've had so much success with them on rooftops."

Plant-by-plant assessment of the two-decade-old garden revealed the inevitable impact of aging. The term dwarf denotes relative, not absolute, size within a given species, and different species grow at different rates; some dwarf conifers top fifteen feet at maturity. Hoerr's analysis identified numerous losses due to increasingly unequal competition for space and sunlight. As a result, he says, "The original design no longer felt cohesive." He sketched the surviving "bones" of the .65-acre garden in black ink to pinpoint anatomical weak spots, and then drew stronger contours over them in red pencil, as guidelines for revision. "Evergreen conifers are pretty static shapes," he explains, "so my edit had to be a four-season exercise in shape and form, with special emphasis on winter. I was really composing architecture." In consultation with CBG staff, Hoerr's team built up a living structure of columns and pyramids, globes and cones—more than 753 examples of 231 conifer taxa.



Because of these plants' distinctive silhouettes and textures, they act as navigational guides to anyone exploring the garden. Hoerr used a full palette of greens, blues, golds, and yellows—"evergreen" conifers are, in fact, far from uniformly green—to mark alluring destinations. He relaxed the landscape's seclusion by opening vistas into the nearby Japanese

Lessons in natural history and horticulture abound at every turn, OPPOSITE, as botanical specimens—from spreading *Juniperus* x *squamata* 'Blue Carpet' to upright *Picea engelmannii* 'Carlson's Red Cone' and pyramidal *Tsuga canadensis* 'Golden Splendor'—flaunt their visual appeal. BELOW: Smaller vignettes offer home-garden takeaways.

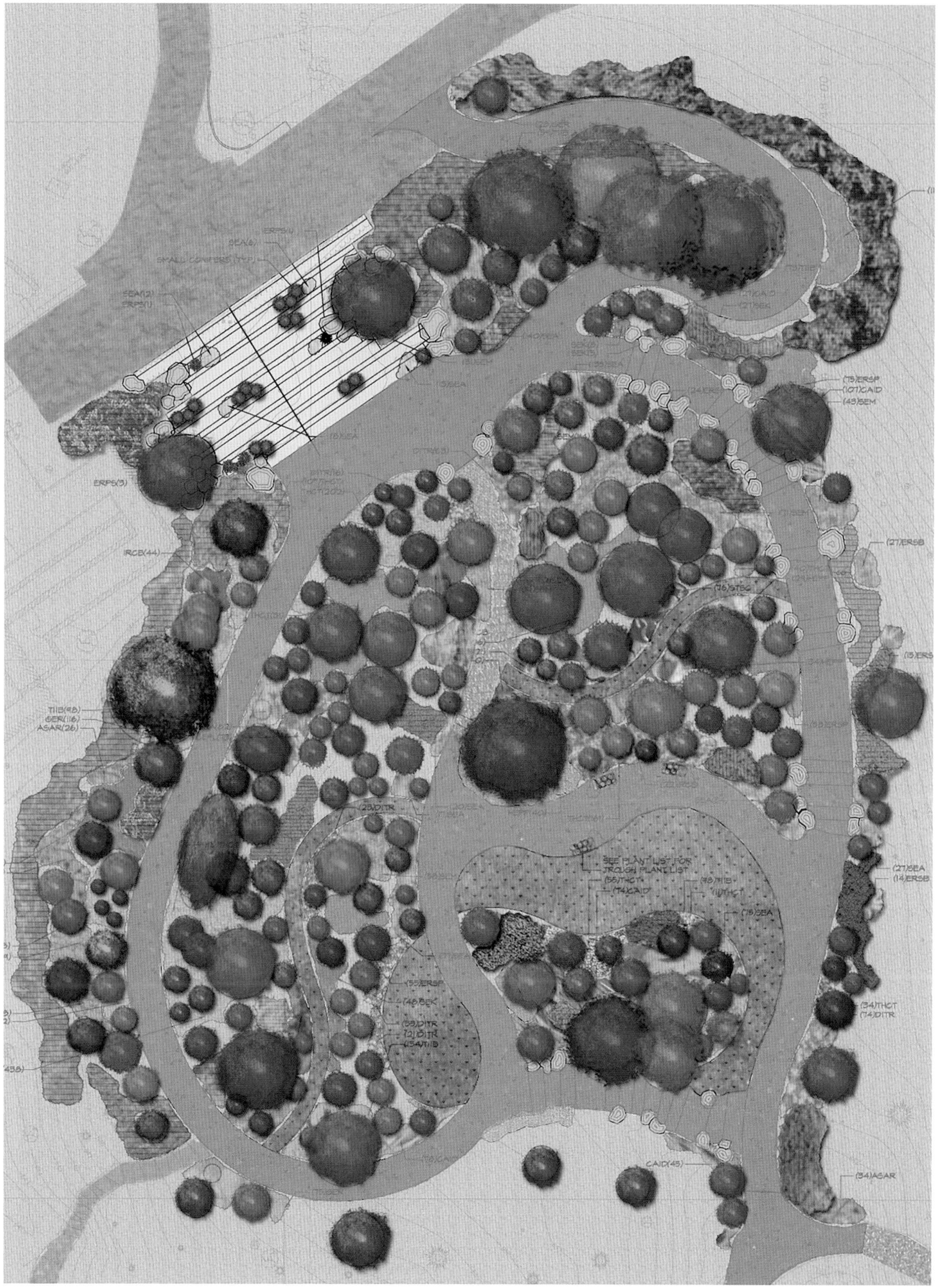

Garden and other areas. To expand accessibility, he eased the climb with a gentle hillside ramp, widened old turf paths, and laid asphalt paving.

No one walking through the Linden Allée today can miss the Dwarf Conifer Garden's new main entrance. Hoerr flags down passersby with a stone staircase of ruggedly magnificent stone; it looks almost like the work of a serendipitous glacier. One linden was removed to clear the view of broad, shallow steps that promise a comfortable-yet-dramatic ascent. Hoerr artfully tucked choice dwarf conifers into pockets amid the limestone risers and crushed-granite treads as though they had taken root by chance, merging architecture into terrain. Each little prodigy begs for a closeup and hints at the bigger thrills upstairs.

OPPOSITE: Dwarf weeping willow (*Salix integra* 'Pendula') and blue spruce (*Picea pungens* 'Glauca Prostrata') drape the foot of a stairway. Although the upright Norway spruce behind them (*P. abies* 'Mucronata') reaches a mature height and width of five feet, it too is considered a dwarf. ABOVE: The boxy silhouettes of the clipped Linden Allée, at right, contrast with the natural cones, globes, and mounds formed by the medley of conifers behind them. RIGHT: An intricate planting plan helped to position each specimen.

Like friendly greeters, diminutive conifers rooted in the gravel entry steps, OPPOSITE, coax visitors to take this gentle uphill detour out of the Linden Allée. Even tinier specimens thrive in small masonry troughs where the path bends above the stairs. ABOVE: Precisely framed views connect the dwarf conifer collection to the Japanese Garden across the lake. LEFT: Snow highlights the garden's robust winter structure.

# Soldier Field

NORTH BURNHAM PARK, CHICAGO 2003

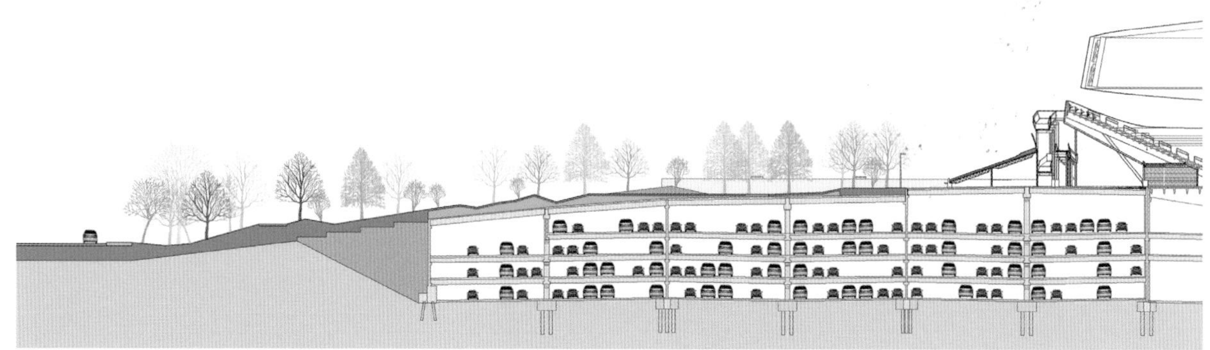

 The usual goals for underground stadium parking—to hide an eyesore, save space, improve sustainability—merely signaled the kickoff at Soldier Field, home of the Chicago Bears. A millennial overhaul of the football club's city-owned stadium in North Burnham Park included the construction of sunken garages, clearing the way for the park to gain seventeen lakefront acres previously squandered on asphalt surface parking lots. The Chicago Park District took full advantage of this chance to have Peter Schaudt "reclaim" the continuous green shoreline envisioned in architect Daniel Burnham's epic 1909 Plan of Chicago.

At the turn of a new century, of course, the City Beautiful Movement had to tackle contemporary challenges. How, for starters, would Schaudt coordinate overlapping layers of vehicular and pedestrian circulation without snarling traffic or spoiling the scenery? How would he fulfill his client's desire for a civic landscape that united—and provided parking for—two hitherto unconnected powerhouses, the McCormick Place convention center, south of the stadium, and the Museum Campus to the north? And how could he make the Bears' front yard a thrilling year-round destination for visitors whose outdoor pursuits range far beyond end zones and LED scoreboards?

Schaudt's winning tactics emerged, quite literally, from a solid ground game. Excavation for the garages—one subterranean, the other partially below grade—yielded more than 120,000 cubic yards of fill, but rather than shoulder the enormous financial and environmental costs of carting soil off site, Schaudt chose to use the found material as his creative medium. He moved earth the way a sculptor models clay. Now grassy hills and valleys undulate over former surface parking lots and across the roof of the 2,500-car underground facility—hidden structural foam supports the nine-acre rooftop garden without exceeding weight restrictions. Paths wend amid multiseason ground covers and groves of trees, for game-day walks, spur-of-the-moment excursions, and visitors sightseeing.

"These rolling landforms energize space and give the sense of seamless terrain," Schaudt said. "Most people don't know if they're standing on terra firma or above somebody's minivan." He added that his man-made dunes distantly reference Lake Michigan's prehistoric topography. This allusion plays well with the nautilus-shaped Children's Garden he carved into a gentle northerly slope. The spiral basin and the spherical art objects it contains relate thematically to exhibits on the nearby campus shared by a natural science museum, an aquarium, and a planetarium. Strolls in the opposite direction—past formal flowerbeds, docks, and a tree-lined parking deck designed for tailgating—lead to the Winter Garden and Sledding Hill. Its forty-foot summit also ranks as a prime location for skyline gazing and other urban spectator sports.

A colossal work of earth art, OPPOSITE, this landscape echoes the twenty-first-century stadium's vast curves as well as the grandeur of the classical facade salvaged from its 1924 predecessor. Next to a spiral Children's Garden, vehicles enter a four-level parking garage sunken below the arena and a rooftop greensward roughly the area of seven football fields, shown in section, ABOVE. Sweeping lawns, BELOW, mask planters for the maples, honey locusts, and elms that heighten the illusion of solid ground.

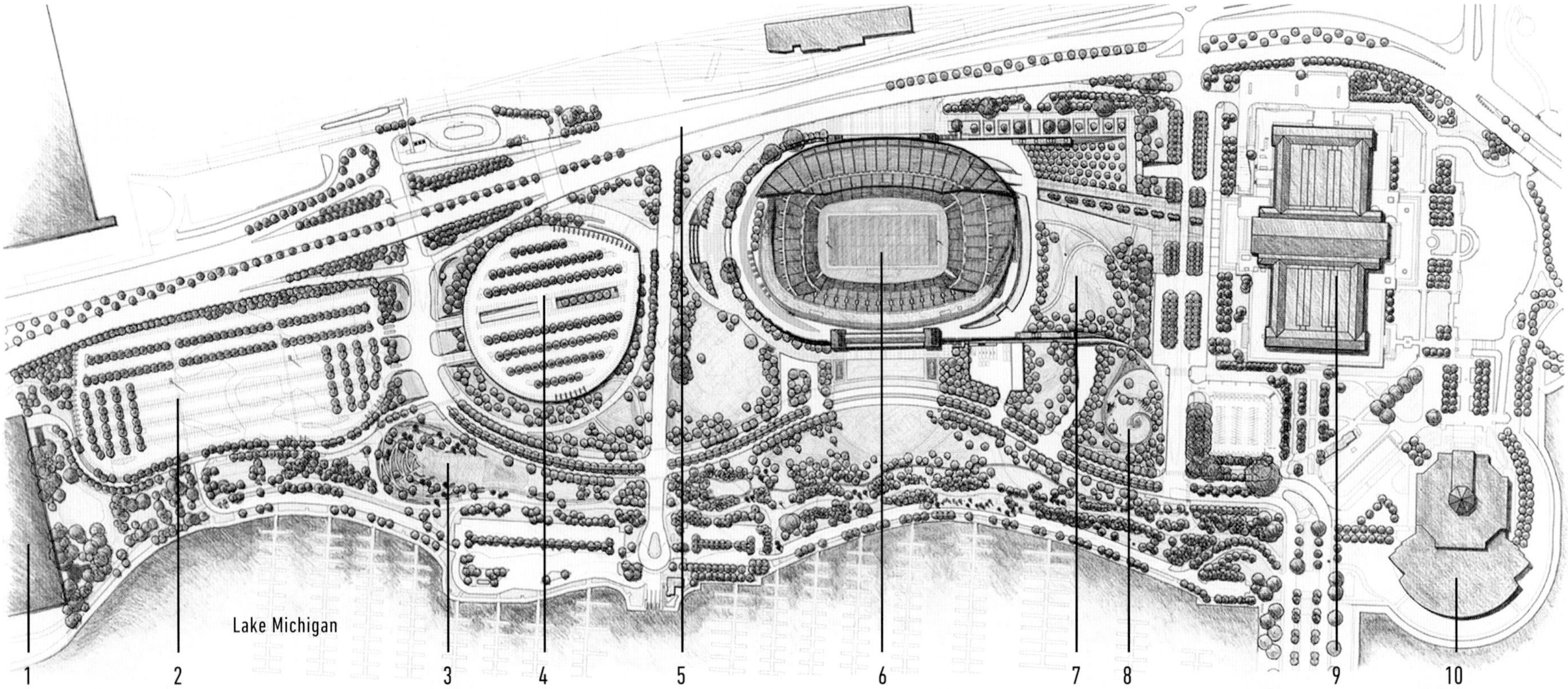

Lake Michigan

1 2 3 4 5 6 7 8 9 10

1. McCormick Place
2. South Parking Lot
3. Sledding Hill
4. Waldron Parking Deck, partially below grade
5. Lake Shore Drive
6. Soldier Field
7. North Parking Structure, underground
8. Children's Garden
9. Field Museum
10. Shedd Aquarium

Spaces for play and education in the Children's Garden, OPPOSITE BELOW, fit into a concave nautilus, a shape that alludes to natural history programs in the nearby aquarium and museum. Outdoor displays within Peter Schaudt's spiral include a model of the moon with brass lunar landing markers, a bronze Earth globe, and a granite "Water Earth." THIS PAGE, BELOW: Colorful prairie plantings and superb views of downtown skyscrapers make the Sledding Hill a year-round magnet for visitors. Actual sleds show up with the first good snowfall.

The stadium's unobtrusively engineered terrain, ABOVE, added seventeen acres of public parkland to Chicago's historic lakefront. The undulating hills and dales were shaped with soil excavated on site, much of which consists of fill recycled from railroad tunnel construction in 1924.

An ideal outdoor room locks architecture and landscape into a tight embrace. Doug Hoerr and Peter Schaudt's exterior living spaces personify that enfoldment, a legacy from their mentors John Brookes and Dan Kiley. The relationships vary markedly from site to site, but the goal is always harmony whether a city house reaches out to claim a patch of bucolic ease amid the metropolis, or a country cousin sets urbane enclosures against a rural panorama. In every setting, though, the designers from both fields have achieved an intimate inside-outside rapport, from carpet to parterre, window mullion to trellis, wing chair to swing.

"I like to concentrate on what you see and feel when you're in a house looking out," says architect Laurence Booth of Booth Hansen, a frequent Hoerr Schaudt collaborator. "I think about standing at a doorway or window and having the space just shoot out as far as it can go." The contours pruned into topiary outside a Booth Hansen facade will always reflect as much scrutiny as the profiles carved into crown moldings on the walls inside.

Conversations between people, plants, and buildings are also the soul of open-air gathering places in nonresidential settings, regardless of differences in scale. The structure of an actual room may be only figurative in a terrace for office workers' breaks, a rooftop garden for neighborhood youth, or an alfresco display area for horticultural marketing, but the comfort of friendly surroundings is palpably real.

# CHAPTER 2 Inside/Outside

Outdoor Rooms

Looking Out

Gathering Places

# Lincoln Park Villa

CHICAGO 2006

In a gravel-carpeted side court tucked between wings of the house, OPPOSITE, 'Whitespire' birches canopy a bronze bench by Kim Hamisky. The stone pavers and pachysandra outline a schematic ground plan, formally dividing this alcove from the play lawn and front fence. ABOVE: Shrubs in curbside parkways tie streetscape to entry garden. PREVIOUS PAGES: Perennials rove through gravel to sketch out casual living areas within the family's private backyard.

It takes street smarts to ease a big, new freestanding house—a true urban villa on a parcel five times wider than Chicago's standard twenty-five-foot residential lot—into the Lincoln Park neighborhood's tight grid. "Our clients talked about a garden where they could enjoy feeling part of the city, the way you do sitting out on a stoop," says Doug Hoerr, who worked on the project hand in hand with architect Laurence Booth. "But, having two young boys, they also wanted to balance urban energy with a comforting sense of enclosure and natural beauty." This dynamic equipoise unites rooms inside the finished house with corresponding roomlike gardens framed by fences, walls, and hedges. Throughout the property, Hoerr, Booth, and interior designer Arlene Semel composed layouts flexible enough to welcome children's games, family meals, and large-scale entertaining. Classical proportions have been honed to a modern edge that focuses deep vistas and defines reassuring boundaries. Exquisitely textured craftsmanship—horticultural and architectural—infuses understatement with nuance.

"When everything's in leaf, you could drive right by and hardly see the house," says Booth. "That was our concept. It just quietly sits in that lush garden." At curb and sidewalk, luxuriant parkway planters and a low, trellis-like iron fence share the scenery with passersby while politely separating the public from private. In the foreground, scattered groves of birch trees soften the precise rectangles of iron fencing, limestone facades and paths, pachysandra beds, and play lawn. The sequence of open-air rooms grows progressively more relaxed as it recedes from the formal entry sequence. In the side yard, for example, a garden court furnished with a sculpture-cum-bench nestles between two wings of the house, hidden from the street but in full view of the central stairway's two-story windows so it can be enjoyed from both indoors and out.

Discreetly tucked behind a magnolia tree and azaleas, a dining terrace adjoins the rear screen porch, which in turn overlooks the most secluded alfresco gathering place. This retreat is a gravel garden, slightly sunken and intriguingly secretive. Free-form plantings wander through the gravel to loosen up the measured geometry all around. A loveseat-scale swing under an arbor and a knee-high fountain pool enhance the mood of casual intimacy, further proof that an idyll can be hip.

The sculptural simplicity of Hoerr Schaudt's custom ipe-wood swing, RIGHT, matches the austere grandeur of architect Booth Hansen's screen dining porch and pergola. Lady's mantle, yucca, and blackberry lily (*Iris domestica*) at ground level, with American wisteria and climbing hydrangea (*Hydrangea anomala* subsp. *petiolaris*) above, temper the ashlar grid of the Wisconsin limestone terrace and pillars. ABOVE: Dainty yellow-flowered kangaroo paw (*Anigozanthos*) shares a pot with strappy clivia near the pergola.

Like a classical colonnade, a row of 'Chanticleer' callery pear trees, LEFT, aligns on axis with a pool in the sunken backyard. Astilbe, hosta, fern, and variegated Solomon's seal flourish in the trees' shade. The water is home to rushes, water lettuce, and papyrus. ABOVE: Vibrant coleus and hosta leaves accent a border.

Composing a white-on-white scheme with the limestone facade, RIGHT, birches light the path from the gravel driveway to the inset front door. Amid pachysandra in the foreground, dusky-leaved bugbane (*Cimicifuga racemosa*) adds a contrasting flourish. ABOVE: An oakleaf hydrangea (*Hydrangea quercifolia*) between the path and sidewalk pokes foliage through the wrought-iron front fence, a Hoerr Schaudt variation on Booth Hansen's geometry.

OPPOSITE, CLOCKWISE FROM BELOW: The tall *Magnolia* x *loebneri* 'Merrill' silhouetted against a curved gable end anchors an open-air sitting room just outside the screen porch. Projecting porch rafters support a green roof that in summer naturally cools the area below it. A round pot brims with plants with arcing leaves, presenting another study in dark and light, round and angular, smooth and rough. Stonecrops such as *Sedum spurium* and *S. spectabile*, interspersed with ornamental onion, make the 320-square-foot green roof a secret garden for enjoyment from upstairs windows.

# Prairie Summer Home

HARBOR SPRINGS, MICHIGAN 2007

At a modern house among old farm fields and woods near Little Traverse Bay, an antique bronze Buddha greets visitors. Doug Hoerr characterizes the artfully natural surroundings he designed for this summer place with what sounds like a Zen koan: "Balancing control and chaos." His clients, a couple with deep roots in Harbor Springs—there's a family nature preserve less than a mile away—love the vast sky, wild horizon, and layered history of Northern Michigan. They are also avid travelers and collectors who prize the eloquent restraint of Asian art. Their ten-acre home base, Hoerr perceived, would need to have a center of gravity as well as fluid boundaries. He found his aesthetic compass in an unexpected neck of the woods: "I thought about how Capability Brown sometimes kept an existing formal garden that was contained by the architecture of the house or elevated on a terrace. From there, people could look out on or step down into his naturalistically styled English countryside."

A New World apart from classical European decorum, the contemporary-style Harbor Springs residence by Rugo/Raff Architects consists of parallel wings linked at one end by a glass entry pavilion. Hoerr enclosed the open end of the central space with a native-stone wall to frame a serene garden courtyard. He built more stone walls to the east and west of the house, projecting its rectangular geometry to create outdoor rooms that survey the rolling terrain. The farther it stretches beyond these orderly enclosures, the less tame the landscape grows. Plantings in distinctly different areas behave accordingly. Clasped by the house, boxwood and pachysandra neatly fit into the entry court's flagstone angles; maples form a symmetrical bosque on the graveled west terrace. Free of architectural restraint, waves of meadow grasses, forbs, and perennials surge across the lawns before drifting into distant banks of native trees.

Unpredictable meetings of yin and yang are arranged with a casual nonchalance that Hoerr calls "planned indifference." The centerpiece of the fastidiously structured entry court is a rough-cut boulder fountain reminiscent of Northern Michigan's abundant artesian wells. Huge window grids offset the gnarled trunks of Amur maples, reminders that early French missionaries knew this region as L'Arbre Croche, "Crooked Tree," their translation of

**The hospitable west terrace, OPPOSITE, adds a major wing to the house. Here, though, the architecture is literally organic: a rectangular bosque of sugar maples spaced to define living and dining areas. Furniture groupings reflect the geometric order of their frame. ABOVE RIGHT: The glass-walled indoor living room looks directly onto the terrace—and through it, to rolling meadow and woods.**

the Odawa tribal name. Water in an oblong reflecting pool, crossed by a bluestone bridge outside the front door, appears to flow under the glass pavilion and feed a meandering stream in back. At one end of the ninety-foot lap pool on the sunken east terrace, high-spirited grasses flood past the stone retaining wall and race all the way to the windowsills of the house. At the pool's opposite end, a goddess statue looks on, unperturbed amid the wind-whipped stalks.

By sunlight, ABOVE, or artificial illumination, BELOW, a red Japanese maple and a twisted Amur maple preside over the entry court's counterpoise of symmetry and asymmetry. OPPOSITE: The saltwater lap pool on the sunken east terrace focuses its own dynamic balance between a lavender wave of Russian sage at left, a shimmering statue dead center, and a weeping Camperdown elm at right.

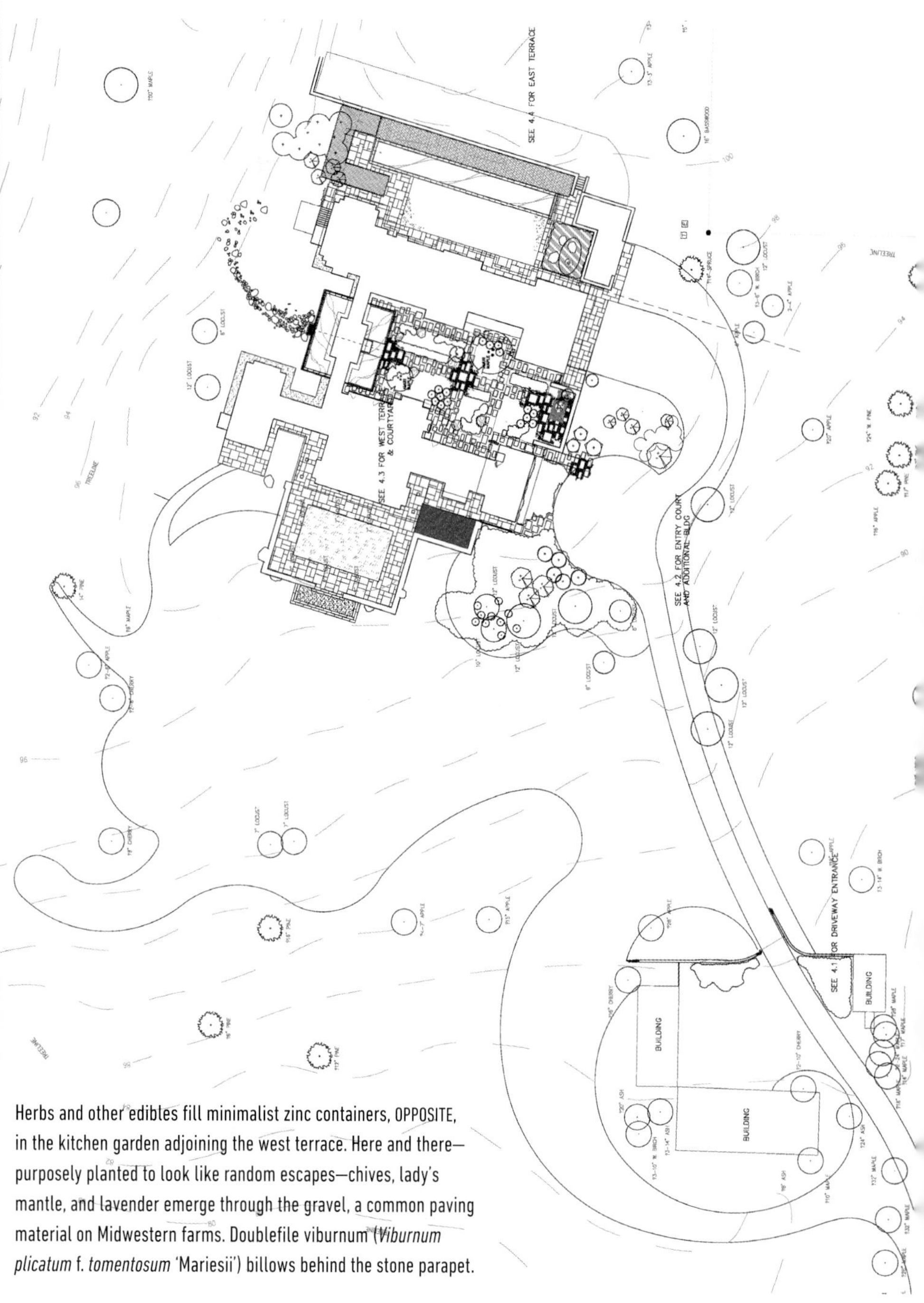

Herbs and other edibles fill minimalist zinc containers, OPPOSITE, in the kitchen garden adjoining the west terrace. Here and there—purposely planted to look like random escapes—chives, lady's mantle, and lavender emerge through the gravel, a common paving material on Midwestern farms. Doublefile viburnum (*Viburnum plicatum* f. *tomentosum* 'Mariesii') billows behind the stone parapet.

Amber waves of switchgrass (*Panicum*) flow in from the aspen grove behind a chaise and umbrella on the east terrace, ABOVE LEFT, as if to assert nature's power by engulfing the walled "room." Meanwhile, on the far side of the house, LEFT, masonry resolutely upholds the designed landscape.

# Classical Walled Garden

CHICAGO 2012



With a deep bow to symmetry, and a sly wink at whimsy, Irish Georgian architecture manages to be both decorous and fanciful. Hoerr Schaudt and architects Booth Hansen tipped their hats to the style in a city residence they designed for a Chicagoan of Irish descent. Because his taste skews traditional—as do vintage houses up and down the block—classical geometry offered an ideal means for achieving indoor-outdoor rapport. Axial vistas link interior and exterior spaces, whether the eye beholds an enfilade of doorways or a maple-tree allée. Fastidiously centered topiaries and fountain jets direct sightlines toward sculptural focal points. Curved garden steps and seating walls respond to the elliptical hall and staircase at the core of the house. A paired open-air fireplace and grilling alcove anchor a terrace as assuredly as mantelpieces inside preside over their domains.

"At every level," Doug Hoerr says, "Larry Booth and I were after the same effect—an air of expectation, the sense that within these aligned spaces something special is about to happen." For this client and his wife, depending on the day's agenda, that something might be a formal party, a spontaneous family get-together, or a moment of pensive solitude. The rational demeanor of a symmetrical landscape is the perfect foil to aesthetic fantasy. On opposite sides of the wife's home office, for instance, canal-like rills extend beyond large windows, producing the mirage of a continuous stream that flows under the floor. One appears to hit a blank stone wall, only to spurt from bronze dolphins into a basin facing the street. On an upper tier behind the rear terrace, a lofty hawthorn hedge performs a metropolitan masquerade while adding greenery to another view: grown in containers atop an alleyway garage, the trees screen out power lines and condos to create the illusion of a private emerald isle.

Not a twig looks out of place in this stately allée of 'Bowhall' maples behind the house, OPPOSITE. The lofty green canopy screens city neighbors, bubbling fountains cancel out urban static, and a stone-lined rill exudes serenity. As straight as the parallel boxwood parterres, the rill centers this vista on a bay window in the home-office pavilion. ABOVE: Paired in front of the Irish Georgian street facade, 'Bloodgood' London plane trees, at curbside, and Washington hawthorns, beside the front door, command a retinue of neatly clipped box.

If the rill, OPPOSITE, were a natural waterway, its "source" would be the rectangular fountain pool outside the former coach house that abuts a back alley. Beds of white impatiens focus sight lines on the shallow niche behind the basin and a bronze naiad by British sculptor Richard Garbe.

To create the illusion that one continuous rill courses through the allée, under the office pavilion, and beyond, Doug Hoerr aligned the rear canal with a twin on the far side of the office, LEFT. Its maple allée reprises the one in back, but the parterre hits a sprightlier note with nesting topiary and blue wishbone flower, *Torenia fournieri*. Water appears to collect in another fountain pool, but then reemerges as spouts from bronze dolphins on the far side of a wall, ABOVE and BELOW, for the delight of passersby.

Sunken below the adjacent allée, the grandly symmetrical rear courtyard, OPPOSITE, relaxes amid feathery honey locust, a weeping European hornbeam (*Carpinus betulus* 'Pendula'), and multitextured beds of shrubs, perennials, and annuals. ABOVE: Potted Meyer lilac standards reflect the curves of steps down from the house. RIGHT: Cotoneaster, daphne, sedge, euphorbia, and dusty miller mingle in a sloped border near the central dining area.

# Residential Views

Since the ancient Romans mastered villa design, no aesthetic means of linking room to room or house to garden has surpassed the classically framed vista. Bilateral symmetry built into an early-twentieth-century Italianate house in Lake Forest, NEAR RIGHT, inspired Doug Hoerr to project an extant axial sightline through the sun porch, OPPOSITE, and out into the new landscape. Renovation by Rugo/Raff Architects and interiors by Athalie Derse compose an elegant vantage point for the long view revealed beyond French doors. 'Annabelle' hydrangeas line a central bluestone path, which skirts a fountain before continuing the promenade through a *Cornus mas* hedge to the swimming pool—a destination as irresistible for the couple with three kids who live here now as it would have been for a patrician *famiglia.*

Thanks to a smooth collaboration among Rugo/Raff, Hoerr Schaudt, and interior designer Tom Stringer, horizontals and verticals form a perfect union at a Northern Michigan house, ABOVE. While furniture keeps a low profile to preserve the view in a master bedroom seating area, dark wood acknowledges the window framing that accentuates the parallel bands of stonework, meadow, woods, and sky outdoors. Neutral upholstery and curtains intensify seasonal color in an adjacent courtyard garden, FAR RIGHT. Spring-flowering *Allium* 'Globemaster' nods above *Panicum virgatum* 'Rotstrahlbusch.'

White stucco creates a picture mat for the vibrant landscape surrounding a Booth Hansen country house in Wheaton, Illinois. CLOCKWISE FROM BELOW: A rustic twig rocker could be a sedate cousin of the tall purple moor grass, *Molinia caerulea* ssp. *arundinacea* 'Skyracer' across the porch windowsill. Other openings frame 'Nearly Wild' roses, cotoneaster, and fountain grass (*Pennisetum*). The view also takes in beds of grasses mixed with coreopsis, *Verbena bonariensis*, and other perennials.

A window-wall garden panorama, BELOW, takes the place of scenic wallpaper or a painted folding screen inside this Northwestern Indiana lake cottage. Plantings on a fifteen-foot dune that shelters the house include astilbe, cotoneaster, daylilies, phlox, hardy geraniums, and heuchera. LEFT: A green roof pulls a floral blanket right up to the bedroom windows, tucking bright annuals in among Solomon's seal, lady's mantle, milkweed, and rodgersia.

An eighteenth-century dancing master would approve the balletic formation of doorways, windows, and furniture that joins the main house to outlying structures and planting beds. In the center hall, BELOW, a pair of loop chairs based on 1930s originals by Frances Elkins, decorator sister of Chicago architect David Adler, echoes the oval-rimmed terrace. LEFT: Pots of tuteur-trained mandevilla across the courtyard perform a symmetrical response.



As orthogonal and refined as the walled garden it surveys, a modern desk, OPPOSITE, makes an ideal partner for new Irish Georgian architecture. Whether viewed from inside or out, the large window's graph-paper-like grid underscores the fastidious balance of its surroundings. Within the office designed—like the rest of the interior—by Roger Ramsay and Michael Syrjanen, desktop objects politely converse with the sculpture and topiaries framed by mullions, lawns, and maple trees.

Dirk Denison Architects set a high bar for sustainability at this Chicago residence, and Hoerr Schaudt's rooftop plantings are essential to meeting the challenge in the dense urban context. Besides replacing street-level green space taken up by the ipe-sided structure, TOP RIGHT, elevated landscapes act as hanging gardens visible from all three stories. TOP LEFT: Aspens and weeping Norway spruce grow above the garage. LEFT and ABOVE: A deck-side "window box" holds juniper, prickly pear, blue spruce, heuchera, and barberry. The roof below supports mixed sedges and alliums.

Glass walls all but evaporate, RIGHT, to maximize views of Lake Geneva from a house in Wisconsin designed by von Weise Associates. In the foreground, Doug Hoerr's fretwork of turf and flagstones extends the building's taut geometry into a plein-air carpet. BOTTOM LEFT: Grassy steps subtly articulate the gradual shift from architecture to parklike terrain. BELOW: Hoerr treated the spaces between von Weise's interlocking pavilions as room-size terrariums for aspens and pachysandra; they further blur the line between indoors and out.

EXIT

# Morningstar Inc.

GREEN ROOF, CHICAGO 2008



"Design permeates everything [at Morningstar], not just the products," Joe Mansueto, the investment research firm's founding CEO, told an Illinois Institute of Technology case study team. "It's the environment, it's the coffee cups, it's the purchase-order forms." This bottom-line priority extends to Hoerr Schaudt's garden terrace for the company's global headquarters, a joint effort with architects Perkins+Will and Gensler. As requested, the nonhierarchical brainstorming that's key to this corporate client's innovative brand migrates easily from open-plan indoor workspaces out onto the green roof. So do coffee breaks. The terrace multitasks as a quiet retreat, a private vest-pocket park seven stories up from the hectic Loop, where employees and visitors can enjoy light refreshment for body and mind.

Because taller buildings surround the garden on all sides and the mechanical-equipment structure below it limited usable surface area to a compact 3,500 square feet, Doug Hoerr took pains to enhance a sense of spaciousness. "We felt that dividing the terrace with anything other than trees, low vegetation, and seating would minimize its scale," says principal Simon Prunty. Instead of ordinary raised planters, everything emerges from a continuous ground plane. "Fortunately," Prunty adds, "early collaboration with the architects allowed us to specify a substantial soil depth for the trees' roots, and the structural loads that would impose." The logistics of high-rise horticulture also gave crane operators a chance to demonstrate their aerial skills.

Searing sunlight bouncing off reflective skyscrapers—and Chicago's relentless wind—triggered the choice of "bullet-proof" honey locusts for the shady canopy above stone benches and a ground cover of hardy *Euonymus fortunei* 'Coloratus,' seasonally varied by bulbs and annuals. Clustering the trees into a tight central grove optically widens the outer paving into a generous podium where chairs can be rearranged for alfresco meetings and parties. Slightly irregular placement of the locust trunks avoids the absolute symmetry of a classic bosque, responding to the garden's relaxed mood and treating individual growth patterns as aesthetic assets. The most devious spatial stratagem here is the clear glass guardrail Hoerr installed, which opens the roof to splendid views of historic landmarks such as the Reliance Building and Marshall Field's. Growth, transparency, perspective—it's enough to make the company's canny investors see green.

**A bosque of the aptly named Skyline honey locust shades the rooftop garden for corporate staff, OPPOSITE. Trees were craned into pits below the terrace floor, RIGHT, so that they appear to grow out of a mechanical penthouse, ABOVE RIGHT.**

Unlike other honey locusts, the Skyline has thornless trunks, a plus when rubbing shoulders with garden visitors. Its resistance to drought, heat, and wind also recommends this variety. 'Globemaster' alliums stand like miniature trees above euonymus dotted with annuals for spring-through-fall color. Glass parapets enhance the effect of floating above the Loop.

# Ball Horticultural

THE GARDENS AT BALL, WEST CHICAGO 2005

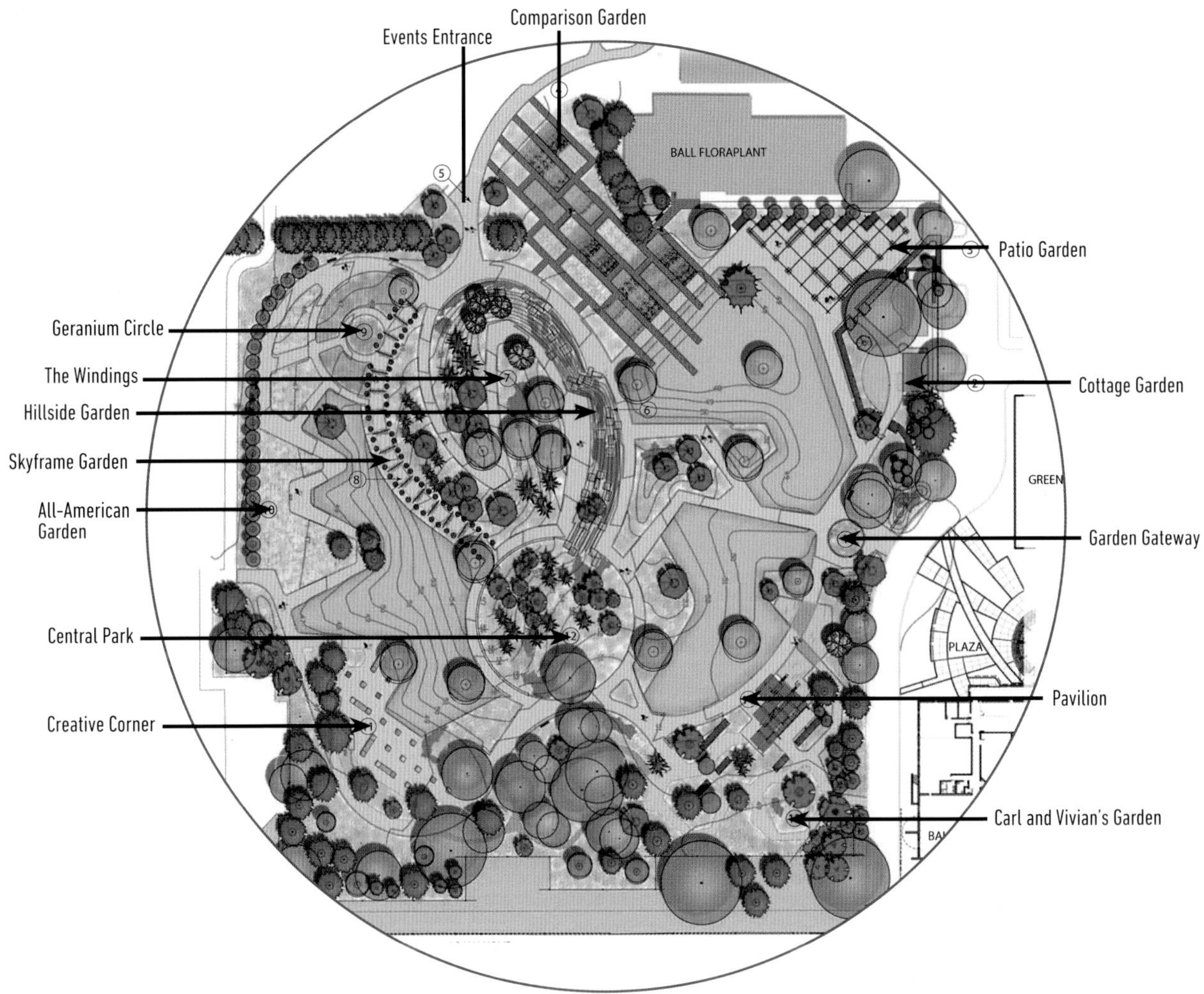


For a moment, Doug Hoerr thought he'd blown the job interview. Anna C. Ball, CEO of the family-owned Ball Horticultural Company—North America's largest wholesale breeder, producer, and distributor of ornamental plants and seed—had just led him through the medley of traditional test gardens outside corporate headquarters. Sprawling "row trial" beds, patched together off and on since 1933, displayed living specimens like 3-D catalog lists. Retailers, landscapers, and other professionals regularly filed through, notebook in hand, to shop the current line for dependable standbys and new releases that might suit their own clients.

"What do you think?" Ball asked Hoerr. "To be honest, Anna, it looks like a miniature golf course." After a moment she replied, "You're hired."

Luckily, the job in question required more candor as well as bold strokes. Ball and her colleagues had concluded that an imaginative, even iconoclastic reinvention of their outdated trial grounds was long overdue. The shock of the new would not only generate fresh interest in a familiar brand—it would affirm a trusted authority's leadership in an industry that Ball's generation had seen evolve beyond the trade of seedsmen like her grandfather George J. Ball, who founded the family firm in 1905. "How products perform in the consumer's garden had become more important than how they do in a trial or on a greenhouse bench," Ball says. "Believe it or not, Doug's vision of looking at plants in the kind of landscape where they're going to end up still seemed like a novel idea to people in this business." The goal was a setting where every visit promised horticultural revelations and sharp new marketing tools to carry home. Ball gave Hoerr free rein over what would eventually amount to nine acres, double the area's former extent. Faced with a tract as flat as a stockroom floor with aisles of green merchandise laid out for taking inventory, Hoerr summoned backhoes to shape rolling topography and winding paths that beg for leisurely strolls. Trees, shrubs, and man-made structures pace a sequence charged with anticipation and surprise while framing each landscape as an episode unto itself. Although aesthetically rewarding, these permanent "showcases for plants," as Hoerr terms them, also deliver sales pitches that can be targeted to changing seasonal priorities. Peak crowds turn up for Ball Seed Field Day and Landscape Day, an industry event held every July. Whether

A color-block bed displays Shock Wave Rose Spreading Petunias in Carl and Vivian's Garden, an area named after second-generation company president Carl Ball and his wife, Vivian Elledge Ball, parents of the current CEO. Offshore, the distinctive foliage of water lilies, water hyacinths, and elephant ears complements this floral profusion.

placidly naturalistic or brazenly theatrical, every stage in the circuit contributes to the promotion of a comprehensive, up-to-the-minute product line. Annuals, perennials, cutting flowers, and vegetables all get their moments in the sun—or shade. Baskets of petunias and other sun lovers hang from a procession of timber Skyframes; more annuals bask in the Hillside Garden's upended concrete culverts. A bright prairie meadow dotted with native species fills Central Park. Shade plants inhabit the Woodlands understory and Patio Garden containers. Were the spirit of George J. Ball to saunter through, he might smile at the Comparison Garden, where hopeful new varieties line up beside honored veterans in Hoerr's rendition of row-trial parades.

OPPOSITE, CLOCKWISE FROM TOP RIGHT: Doug Hoerr turned blocky concrete culverts on end to fashion colossal containers for annuals beside steps into the Hillside Garden. Formal Victorian carpet bedding takes a modern turn with polka dots of flowers. Landscape Day attendees stroll beneath petunias, scaevola, and dichondra hung from a few of the seventeen Skyframe arbors. A stone retaining wall guides visitors toward The Windings, a path to the panoramic lookout on the garden's highest ground.

THIS PAGE, FROM TOP: Skyframes escorted by low *Arborvitae* 'Woodward's Globe' show off hanging containers of begonias, petunias, sweet potato vine, and other annuals. Hoerr's concrete "plinths" convert the traditional row-trial pattern into minimalist sculpture near the arbor-like Patio Garden for shade-loving plants. Containerized petunias and cleome overlook Ball's naturalistic Central Park, where meadow-like drifts of yellow-flowering bidens and pink gomphrena mix with ornamental grasses.

On broad shallow steps comfortably pitched for browsing, OPPOSITE, professional shoppers get to peruse products like nasturtiums and zinnias. Woody plants outside the Ball range, such as staghorn sumac and mugo pine (left), contribute a lasting structure for the frequent rotation of annuals.

THIS PAGE, FROM TOP LEFT: Golden bidens bloom in front of the Pavilion for corporate entertaining designed by Woodhouse Tinucci Architects. Groves of red maples dignify the walk from the main building to the Garden Gateway. Ornamental millet, rudbeckia, and pennisetum weave a prairie-like fringe below a cavalcade of Skyframes.

OF THE

# Gary Comer Youth Center

GREEN ROOF, CHICAGO 2007

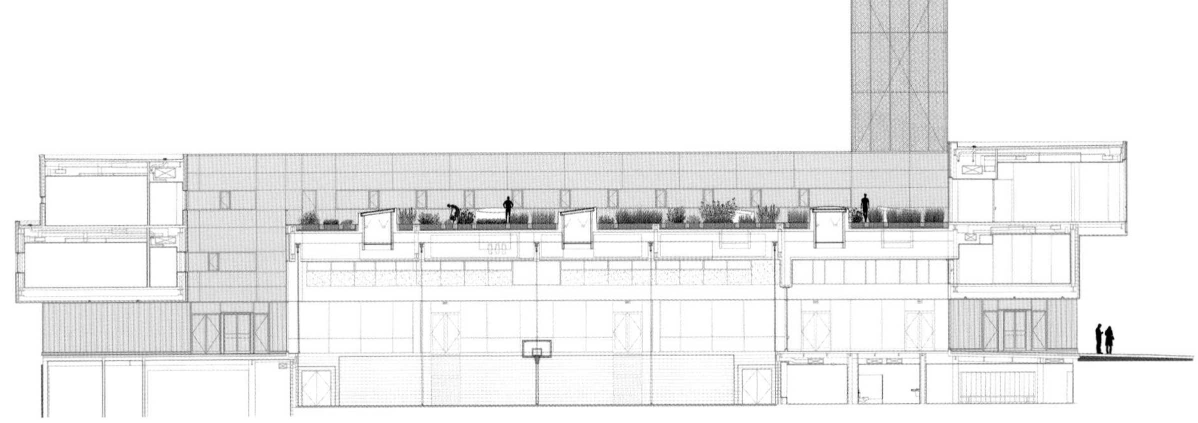



Safe, friendly environments for after-school programs like the Gary Comer Youth Center's are precious few in Grand Crossing, a low-income community on Chicago's South Side. Rarer still are secure, inviting outdoor spaces like the Center's green roof, a garden atop a two-story gymnasium where local children and teenagers learn to cultivate organic vegetables, herbs, and flowers. "These kids have never planted a seed before, let alone helped it grow into something tasty to eat for lunch," said Peter Schaudt. He designed the garden in close collaboration with architect John Ronan and donor Gary Comer, a Grand Crossing native who founded the retailer Lands' End.

Comer welcomed Schaudt's suggestion that capital costs include the employment of a full-time garden manager, not only to supervise hands-on activities, but also to demonstrate their relevance to biology, horticulture, and nutrition. The project budget also stretched to afford a structure capable of supporting soil eighteen to twenty-four inches deep. Almost triple the depth—and weight load—of typical nonagricultural green roofs, this volume is required to nurture food crops as diverse as potatoes, carrots, strawberries, and lettuce.

"A wonderful thing about this green roof," Schaudt said, "is that you're up off the streets, but you don't feel like you're on a roof. You're in a courtyard." Glass-walled classrooms and corridors overlook the garden on all sides, keeping everyone at the Center in touch with their on-site, working farm. Ambient heat from the upper story, warmth from the gym and café downstairs, and solar energy put the sheltered planters into a more temperate climate zone than the surrounding neighborhood. Floating row covers protect winter crops from damaging frost. Almost-continuous growing seasons enable the 8,160-square-foot patch to yield at least 1,000 pounds of produce every year. In addition to generating camaraderie, self-confidence, and pride, harvests teach entrepreneurial lessons: freshly picked edibles that aren't gobbled up in the Center's café get sold to Chicago restaurants.

Another wonderful thing about this green roof is the graphic punch of its colorful stripes. Schaudt and Ronan's exact alignment of horizontal crop rows and flower beds with vertical facades presents a case study in artistic minimalism and practical sustainability. Plastic lumber made from recycled milk cartons frames the planters; recycled-tire pavers surface the paths. Cylindrical metal skylights protrude from the gym and café like abstract sculptures in a modernist potager, syncopating the regular rhythm underfoot.

Speaking to youngsters and staff at the Center in May 2012, First Lady Michelle Obama praised, "this thriving, inspiring, beautiful place, just minutes from where I grew up." She cited the many educational opportunities available there for the pursuit of fresh interests and future careers, from broadcasting and culinary arts to politics. "If you want to be a scientist," she said, "then get up on top of that roof and start studying those plants and working in that garden . . . which, by the way, is more than five times bigger than the garden at the White House. I'm not hating on you, but you've got us far outmatched."

**Sheltered on all four sides within the center's top story, crops and gardeners benefit from a man-made microclimate, OPPOSITE. Tools were specially designed for cultivating the green roof's eighteen-inch soil depth, LEFT.**

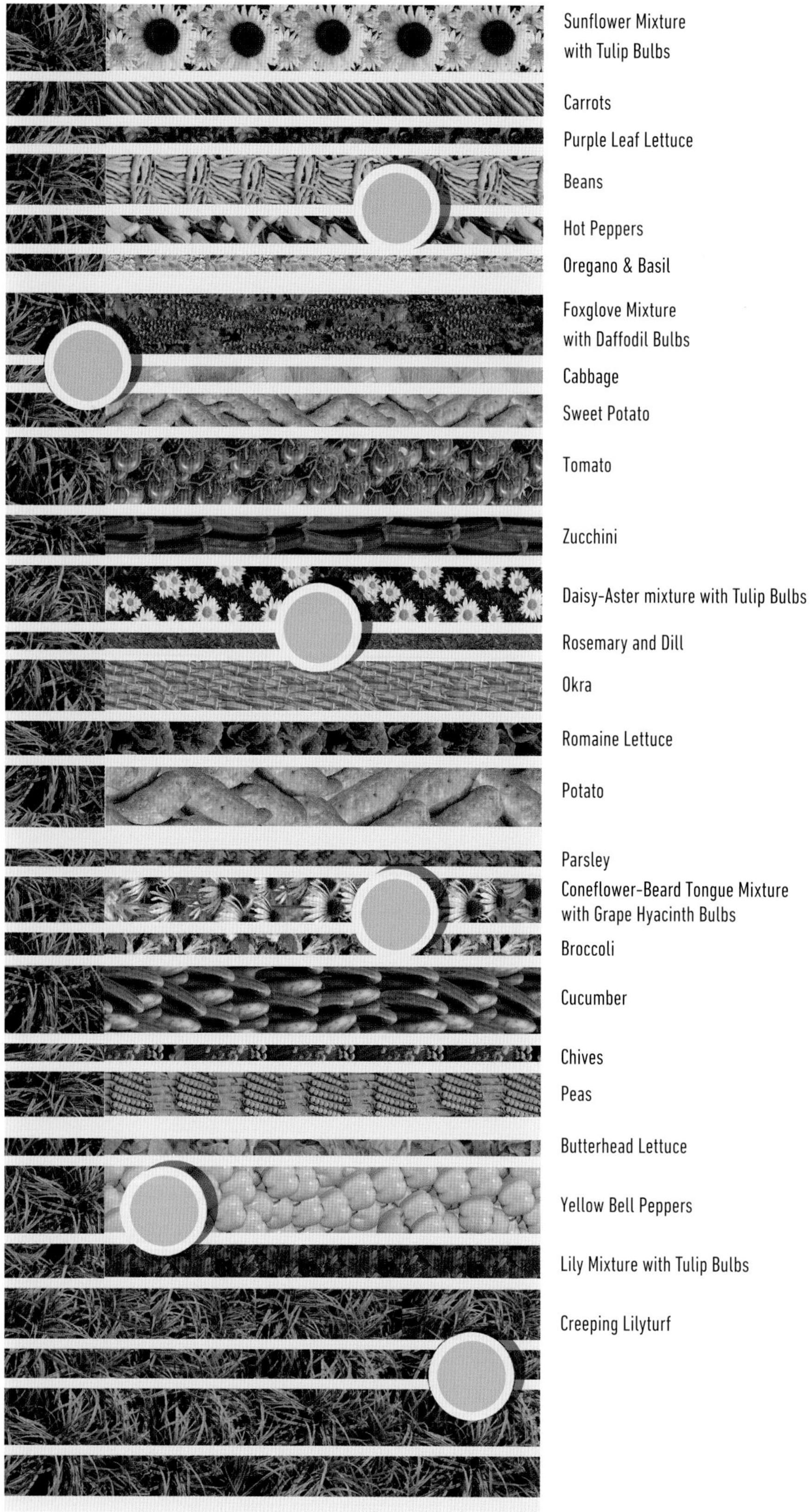

Sunflower Mixture with Tulip Bulbs

Carrots

Purple Leaf Lettuce

Beans

Hot Peppers

Oregano & Basil

Foxglove Mixture with Daffodil Bulbs

Cabbage

Sweet Potato

Tomato

Zucchini

Daisy-Aster mixture with Tulip Bulbs

Rosemary and Dill

Okra

Romaine Lettuce

Potato

Parsley

Coneflower-Beard Tongue Mixture with Grape Hyacinth Bulbs

Broccoli

Cucumber

Chives

Peas

Butterhead Lettuce

Yellow Bell Peppers

Lily Mixture with Tulip Bulbs

Creeping Lilyturf

In classic potager style, edibles alternate with ornamentals, LEFT. The selection and planting of vegetables and herbs, bulbs and flowers are staged for the longest possible growing season. TOP: Besides gaining experience in organic food production, young gardeners taste the fruits of their labor, as prepared by chefs in the center's café downstairs. Chicago restaurants also buy the Center's produce, giving hands-on lessons in marketing and customer relations.

John Ronan Architects purposely insulated the fertile outdoor classroom from street-level distractions, ABOVE. Frequent encounters with birds, insects, and earthworms broaden city children's horizons. A bird's-eye view emphasizes the graphic pattern of garden crop rows and paths.

The stylish utility of circular skylights for the gym/performance hall below is just the thing for a modern urban farm surrounded by glass, ABOVE. Sleek metal framing sets off meadow-like clumps of coneflower, catmint, liatris, penstemon, and dill. Thanks to transparent walls, horticultural activities are constantly visible to students and administrators inside the building. White recycled-plastic paths are spaced so that crops can be tended without compacting the lightweight soil.

Participants in other Center programs, such as this girl matching colors for an art project, LEFT, have access to the garden too. Out of sight below the vegetation and soil, the entire plot rests on a structural concrete slab topped with insulation and waterproofing, water-retentive plastic drainage plates, and a double layer of protection against damage from overenthusiastic digging.

# Uptown Normal Circle

NORMAL, ILLINOIS 2011

Parents urge their kids to play in this traffic circle, just as Peter Schaudt said they would. From his first meeting with community leaders in Normal, Illinois, population 52,000, to discuss upgrading a treacherous five-way crossroads into a rotary, he could tell that usual rules would not apply. As the focal point of an LEED redevelopment plan by architects Farr Associates for Normal's struggling central business district, the circle was expected to meet high ecological goals while providing a hub for economic growth, cultural activities, transit, and recreation. "Normal didn't set out to go 'crazy West Coast green,'" Schaudt said, "but after a ton of public meetings, they had the vision to keep sustainability up front—an exceptional commitment for a midsize American town anywhere." A year after its completion, the Uptown Normal Circle won an Environmental Protection Agency National Award for Smart Growth. Private companies have invested $160 million in the surrounding district, and retail sales have risen 46 percent.

Schaudt was adamant that this roundabout not turn into a speedway with some ornamental eye-catcher in the middle. "Louis XIV would plunk down a giant sculpture in a rond-point as a control

**Normal's plaza is at once an outdoor living room for the whole town, a gateway and hub for visitors, and a spot where everyone dips a toe or finger into sustainable design. RIGHT: London plane trees overhang the inner fountain ring and the concentric bog planted with iris, cattails, and rushes.**

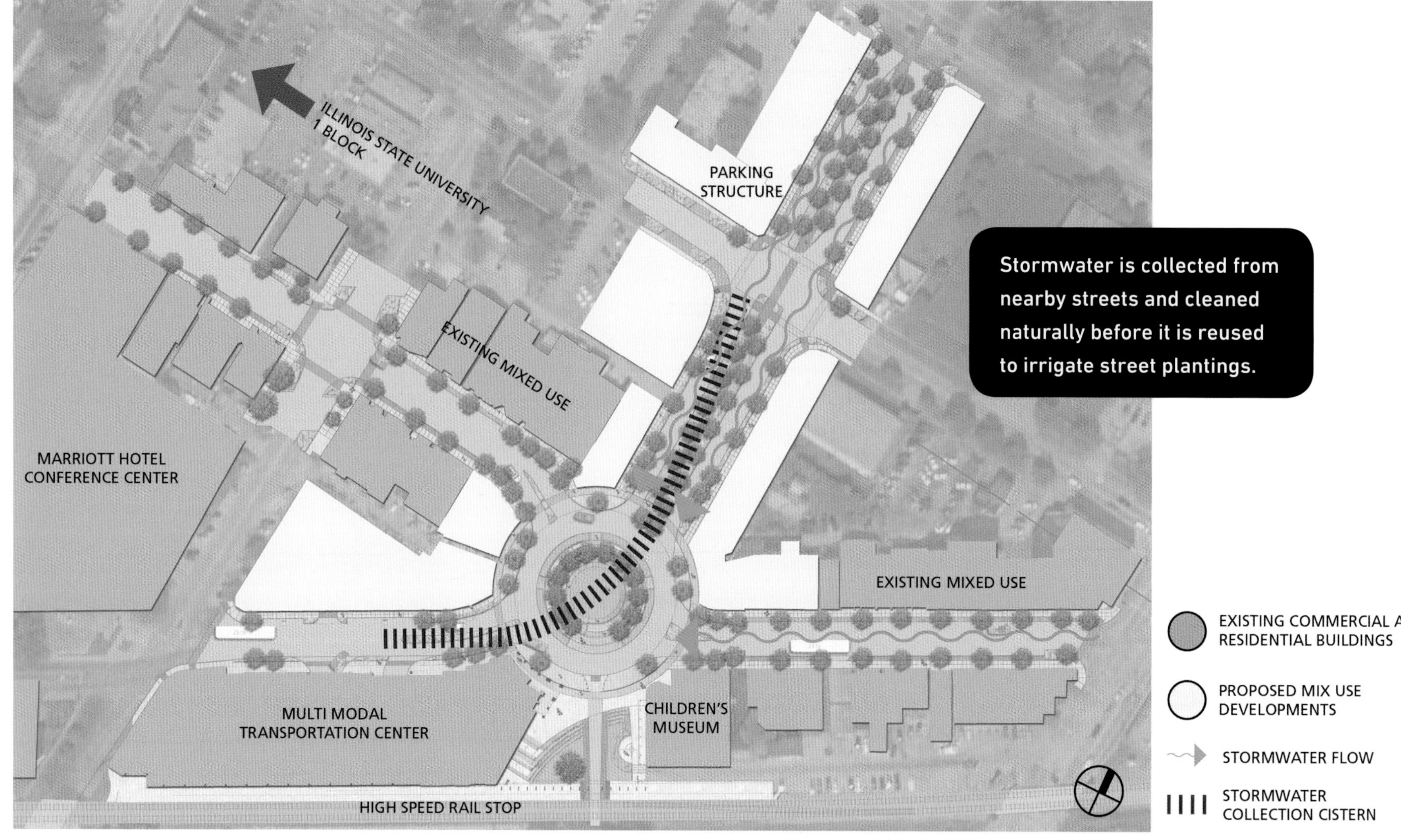


mechanism," Schaudt said. "A modern society shouldn't define its center with a Civil War statue. No, make it an open space for people to enjoy as they want. Make it a place, not a thing. A verb, not a noun." Although vehicles are granted passage through Normal's curb-free plaza, the single-lane, right-turn-only roadway slows traffic to a safe pace for pedestrian crossings. Office workers and shoppers, young families and college students, cyclists and joggers converge on Uptown Normal's own Central Park—the close neighbors it connects include a transit station, a children's museum, a multiuse trail, and a university campus. The lure is a lounge-worthy lawn ringed by benches, shade trees, and a curved fountain-canal with low embankments and shallow cascades ideal for wading—or for pondering ecosystems.

On-site drainage studies and historical finds—the bed of a diverted prairie creek and a vast, disused sewer—helped guide Schaudt to the idea of making natural stormwater recycling a cause for public celebration. The process begins out of sight with the collection of runoff from three adjacent streets in a 75,000-gallon underground cistern, aka the repurposed sewer. Some of that water feeds irrigation lines for neighborhood turf and trees. The rest gets pumped into elegant "bogs" near the Circle's rim, to be cleansed by aquatic plants before circulating through a subterranean UV filter and finally splashing into the canal designed for fun, relaxation, and remembrance of the bygone creek. Schaudt commanded this waterway to flow counterclockwise, mirroring the stream of cars and buses and muffling engine noise.

More often than not, laughter, chatter, and music drown out intrusive sounds. The plaza layout is geared to accommodating picnics and other casual get-togethers, as well as scheduled events like a blues festival, a bike rodeo, and holiday caroling. After hearing that Occupy Wall Street supporters had camped out there, Schaudt remarked, "It's one more sign that the new Normal has arrived."

THIS PAGE, COUNTERCLOCKWISE FROM BOTTOM LEFT: In the "bog," aquatic plants such as water hyacinth collect toxins and remove sediment and debris from stormwater runoff pumped from an underground cistern. The splashes and ripples that call out to waders also tone down traffic sounds. Purified water cascades into the fountain rivulet.

OPPOSITE: With each pass through the efficient sand, UV, and bog filter system, storm water is naturally cleansed of an estimated 91 percent of total suspended solids, 79 percent of phosphorus, and 64 percent of nitrogen. A study by the Landscape Architecture Foundation noted that the Circle's trees absorb about 10,790 pounds of carbon a year—the amount generated by one car over the same time.

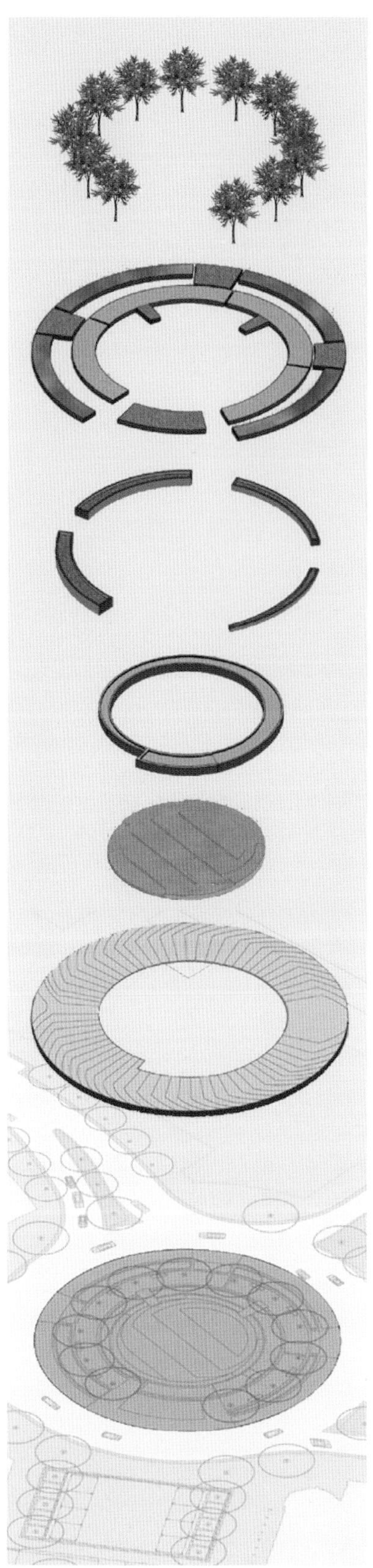

Tree Enclosure

Outer Lawn
and Promenade

Bog Filters

Fountain

Central Lawn

Topography

The boundaries set in a deed often fall short of measuring real estate's true dimensions. A panorama of mountain peaks far beyond legal property lines, a glimpse of treetops in a yard next door—through skillful framing, either view perceptually enlarges the given vantage point. "Peter and I have always looked for inspiration in the greater landscape to which a specific site belongs," Doug Hoerr says. "You honor the larger place, even when you need to create privacy within it."



Reliance on indigenous plants and regional landforms strengthens ecological as well as visual bonds between a new design and its environs. Traditional patterns and materials—grids laid out by territorial surveyors and city planners, split-rail fences and native-stone walls—root an individual garden or even a green roof in the broad substrate of social and cultural shifts. A raised terrace or a man-made mount sharpens perspective on ground-level complexities. An allée insists that a skyscraper join a garden stroll. A corporate pavilion lends an ear to restless prairie grasses.

Water delineates the edges of landscapes as effectively as it blurs them. Even in projects of quite different scale and purpose, a rill and a river, a pond and a lake can reflect the dreamer in each of us with stunning clarity. A designer who shapes a shore or a bridge can channel the force of imagination.

# CHAPTER 3 What Lies Beyond

Embracing Environs

At Water's Edge

# SandRidge Energy Commons

OKLAHOMA CITY 2013



"Spending time outdoors in Oklahoma City can feel like an endurance sport," Peter Schaudt said. Extreme temperatures, relentless wind, and frequent tornadoes come with the territory. SandRidge Energy, an oil and natural gas company, was nonetheless determined to create outdoor space at its new headquarters. Because the site, a full city block, lay at the crossroads of an ongoing downtown revival, civic-minded management ruled out a conventional, hermetically sealed skyscraper and corporate plaza. Instead, they chose to adaptively reuse important historic structures—the 1923 Braniff Building and a 1967 tower by Pietro Belluschi—and open the ground in between to multiseasonal enjoyment by the public as well as SandRidge employees. Then-CEO Tom Ward asked that Hoerr Schaudt and Rogers Partners not even refer to it as a campus. Ward preferred the term commons: "We wanted to share with our neighbors. We didn't want to set up walls."

Open space, of course, has its downside for city dwellers realistically concerned about being blown away. Hoerr Schaudt pored over weather patterns and conducted a barrage of studies, including a wind-tunnel model, to determine the profile for climatic exposure within these 3.5 acres. Happily, research also yielded an efficient and attractive stratagem proven by generations of Oklahoma farmers: "shelterbelts," bands of trees planted as windbreaks, which date back to the Dust Bowl era of the 1930s. Schaudt's design team buffered the vulnerable southern edge of the SandRidge grounds with an innovative shelterbelt that staggers alternating rows of evergreens and deciduous trees across a steep, man-made berm.

For pedestrian access at a gentler gradient, entrance paths skirt the slope diagonally, banked by drought-tolerant perennials and native grasses that dance in the breeze. "The experience unfolds as you ascend," Schaudt noted. "It's a little bit like the

The restless winds of the Great Plains ruffle native grasses even within the architectural framework of downtown, OPPOSITE and PREVIOUS PAGES. Green spaces and paths, BELOW, multitask as corporate campus and public commons.

excitement you feel climbing to the Acropolis." The oblique angles of ramps and stairs also foreshadow the crisscross walkways and tilted lawn that make the inner landscape a rhythmic counterpoint to the surrounding street grid. Rogers Partners' soaring canopy, which deflects sun and wind, resounds to alfresco performances and gatherings. Only insiders will discern an oblique allusion elucidated by Hoerr Schaudt project manager Michael Skowlund: "The angular design language of both the landscape and the architecture evolved in part from a study of the molecular structure of methane, an important gas in our client's industry."

More straightforwardly, the northern segment of the site calls up the rocky regions of Oklahoma and Texas where SandRidge bases most of its operations. Jagged, abstract landforms at company headquarters blossom with indigenous blanket flower, black-eyed Susan, and meadow sage. One verdant plane bends downward to flank the entrance ramp for underground parking. Conscious that, as Skowlund says, "No one likes driving down into a dark hole," Hoerr Schaudt anchored the descent with a grove of mature loblolly pines. Like trusty guides, the trees signal that nature can be a source of reassurance.

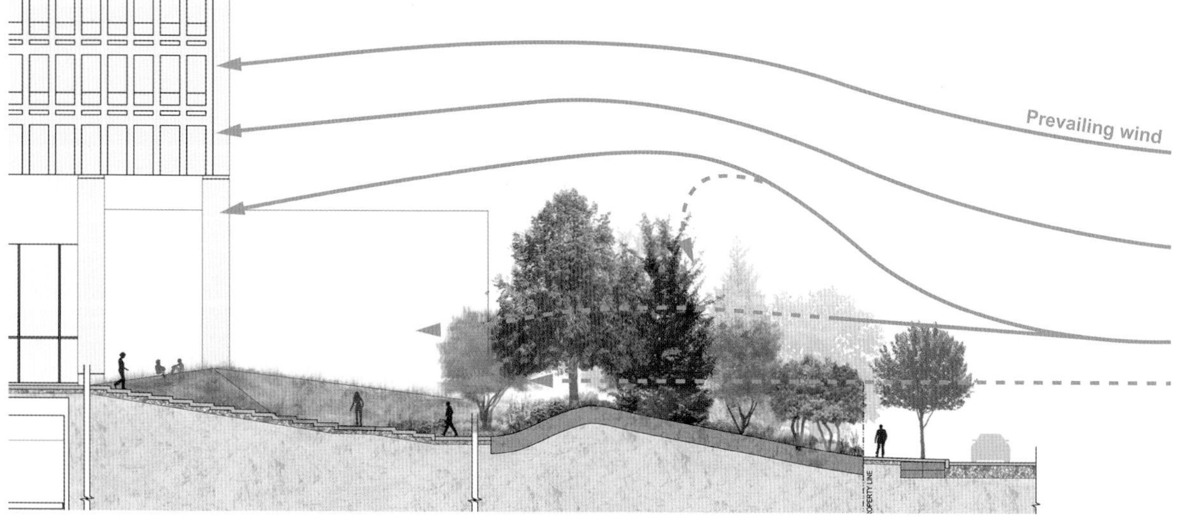


Given a site at the core of Tornado Alley, Hoerr Schaudt devised an urban version of a rural shelterbelt along the most vulnerable, southern edge of the block, ABOVE LEFT. Peter Schaudt sculpted the land and planted tree windbreaks of evergreen and deciduous trees, staggering Blue Atlas cedars, oaks, and other species as they climb the slopes below Pietro Belluschi's landmark tower. LEFT: Leeward protection from gusts extends to a distance ten times the height of the tallest tree.

Berms constructed as midblock wind buffers, OPPOSITE, also carve out attractive gathering places. Along a ridge in the foreground, drought-tolerant sedums, alliums, and hardy geraniums weave a textural tapestry that helps to filter gusts. Behind the seating wall, native Indian grass (*Sorghastrum nutans*) wanders through heat-resistant loblolly pine (*Pinus taeda*) and river birch (*Betula nigra*) 'BNMTF' Dura-Heat.

3/29/10 PWS

Rogers Marvel's sun-and-wind canopy, OPPOSITE ABOVE, flares over the plaza's central terrace, next to the 1923 Braniff Building, another historic structure the architects adapted for the SandRidge complex. OPPOSITE BELOW, FROM LEFT: A Schaudt sketch abstracts the play of verticals and horizontals that energizes the descent into underground parking. Loblolly pines make improbably suave companions to Pietro Belluschi's columns on the adjacent structure.

THIS PAGE, COUNTERCLOCKWISE FROM TOP LEFT: Brushing up against an angular bench, supple Mexican feathergrass (*Nassella tenuissima*) catches the slightest breeze. Fixed seating in windy spots yields to movable furniture in more sheltered areas. Rectilinear paving maintains tectonic order amid tough vegetation. Fair-weather cyclists pass a heat- and ice-resistant juniper (*Juniperus virginiana* 'Canaerti') on the right.

# New England Farm

PORTSMOUTH, RHODE ISLAND 2016



Dream clients for domestic landscapes thrive on a change of scenery, whether that means walking from one garden bed to the next or traveling between far-flung estates. Consider the Van Beuren family, residents of Philadelphia's Main Line who also have a summer farm in Rhode Island and a winter retreat on the island of Antigua. Hoerr Schaudt's designs for their seasonal getaways respond to radically different habitats. The contrasts, however, only emphasize familial traits shared by both landscapes: a love of nature and regional tradition; a taste for low-key comfort and relaxed entertaining; a delight in greenery, calm colors, long views, and discreetly sprung surprises.

The sixty acres that the Van Beurens bought in Rhode Island came with charmingly weathered shingle buildings—and a prize of a 360-degree sweep of pristine coastal countryside unfolding like a Luminist painting. "Looking across neighbors' farms, you see the unbroken history of a rural vernacular," says Doug Hoerr. For all its local color, though, the site lacked cohesive structure. The main house, guest cottage, vegetable patch, and tennis court seemed loosely scattered among the open fields. "Our goal," Hoerr says, "was to enhance the beauty already here by creating a sense of progression, scale, and discovery." His design team used vernacular idioms to give their thorough edit a tone of unrevised authenticity.

Mature trees were planted along the entrance drive to dignify it as a rustic allée. The patterning of split-rail fences and granite gateposts, fieldstone walls and paths, hedges and grass-and-gravel lanes punctuates the residential compound. Boundary lines as neat as crop rows parse distinct areas, such as the donkey paddock and the enlarged cutting garden. Billowy shrubs and perennials soften transitions and gently shape intimate enclosures. Some of the subtlest enhancements in Hoerr Schaudt's master plan belie the heavy lifting they entailed. Take the party barn, a c. 1850 antique

**The antique barn, which looks as though it has weathered in place for a century or more, OPPOSITE, was actually shipped here in pieces from Connecticut. Other recent additions to the seemingly timeless landscape include a 'Limelight' hydrangea hedge and sycamores etching the sky. RIGHT: Selective tree culling and transplanting artfully "borrowed" views beyond the property lines.**

that Hoerr had architect Eric J. Smith dismantle in Connecticut and reconstruct west of the parking court. East of the main house, full-grown trees were culled or transplanted and vast swathes of earth recontoured as greensward, transfiguring piecemeal glimpses of Narragansett Bay into a panoramic vision of Arcadia.

Two-track gravel-and-grass drives, dry-laid fieldstone walls, split-rail fences, and cross-braced gates, OPPOSITE, rework regional precedents. Near the barn, Allegheny viburnum, Hoogendorn holly, and catnip round a bend. ABOVE: Gravel and flagstones supply rustic texture to the parking court. White-flowering *Hydrangea arborescens* 'Annabelle' and *H. paniculata* 'Tardiva' soften the edges with cottage-garden fullness. RIGHT: On the main house's east terrace, masses of deep green foliage anchor dainty pink 'The Fairy' roses and purple verbena.

1 Copse
2 Tennis court
3 Vegetable/cutting garden and orchard
4 Guest cottage and gravel garden
5 Sunken lawn with water feature
6 Main house
7 East terrace
8 Mixed borders
9 Parking court
10 Barn
11 Donkey paddock
12 Woodland tunnel
13 Expanded woodland
14 Restored historic drive

OPPOSITE, CLOCKWISE FROM TOP RIGHT: Relaxed formality gently focuses this stone walk on a pastoral prospect of elm trees and turf. A magnolia shelters the cedar-shingled guest cottage. The shingled garage supports an espaliered pear tree. Donkeys graze in the paddock Hoerr built for them. On the uphill side of the adjacent barn (donkeys enter lower-level stalls downhill), a ramp leads to lofty interiors retooled for casual entertaining. THIS PAGE, BELOW LEFT: Serpentine mixed borders of annuals and perennials brim with alyssum, lobelia, sedum, lady's mantle, salvia, cleome, and cosmos. BELOW RIGHT: 'Nikko Blue' hydrangeas show the way to Hoerr's rendition of a classic New England spindle gate.

En route to the wisteria arbor and garage off the parking court, OPPOSITE, stepping-stones pass a quietly opulent mound of heuchera and variegated dogwood. Across the path, airy *Verbena bonariensis* leans over a clematis-draped stone wall. LEFT: A handsomely utilitarian greenhouse overlooks the vegetable and cutting garden. Kitchen crops and flowers grow in raised beds as well as in the ground. The elbow of a wall frames cleome, snapdragons, and zinnias.

Fieldstone and manicured box, LEFT, define the long, straight promenade from house to tennis court. Blueberry bushes ring a dogwood beside the wall. TOP RIGHT: A brief but incandescent flash of spring color ignites the lawn when grape hyacinths bloom under a horse chestnut. ABOVE: A flat, unbroken lawn originally occupied the area where a sunken water feature today nurtures cattails and lily pads. Rhododendrons reinforce romantic seclusion.

# Island Retreat

ANTIGUA, WEST INDIES 2016

Antigua's desert-island palette ranges from palm-studded shoreline washed by turquoise surf to inland tracts of parched sandy soil and scrub. Both ends of this spectrum, the seductive and the prickly, exist within the five-acre Van Beuren property. A long drive cuts straight through arid indigenous terrain on its way to the house—actually an indoor-outdoor complex of pavilions and garden courtyards—which shelters out of sight between the base of a steep hill and the beach. Extrovert and introvert mingle in buildings and man-made landscapes that alternately embrace this complex environment and hold it at arm's length.

Arriving guests are met by a simple archway—the true front door—in a high, native-limestone wall whose reserve only magnifies the lavish welcome of the garden inside. "This outdoor entry hall, artfully furnished with lush tropical shrubs, vines, and perennials, signals a different experience from the scrubland at your back," Hoerr says. "It also amps up the eureka moment when you turn, look through the living room, and . . . Wow, there's the sea!" Sculptural trees like gumbo limbo adorning the interior courtyards are, in some cases, found art original to the site, which the designers selectively retained and pruned. The spatial sequence articulated by richly textural new plantings, as well as subtly rhythmic paving and fountains, establishes a strong tectonic order. The masterstroke is an axial

A discreet presence on its bayside shoreline, LEFT, the family compound keeps a low profile behind dunes lush with beach naupaka, sea grape, and palms. ABOVE: Views by land only begin at Hoerr Schaudt's entry gate, with a glimpse of the house past a courtyard walk lined with wart fern and spider lily. The pitted surface of salt finish-concrete paving, beyond the arch, blends well with native-stone walls.

vista Hoerr Schaudt plotted through the very heart of the compound.

At one end of this sightline, strategically added palms play up the reveal of the beach. At the opposite end, facing inland, a stone garden staircase ascends into dense vegetation. "The steps say, 'Okay, we're heading back into the wild now!'" Hoerr explains. "You can't see what's up there but you know that some exciting destination beckons." Few can resist a climb into the jungle, where a path rises to a lattice-roofed lookout in a clearing high above the coast. Even veteran globetrotters who shun the phrase "tropical paradise" have declared the treetop views of sky and water heavenly.

Inside the entry court, OPPOSITE, flashes of turquoise through tropical foliage and open pavilions are visitors' first sight of the sea. Sinewy branches gesture behind callistemon, ixora, puncturevine, and bromeliads.

Potted plants arranged as "borders" in the gravel garden off the court, ABOVE, stand ready for transport to other parts of the landscape on demand. ABOVE LEFT: To enliven bare walls in the breezeway outside the dining pavilion, Doug Hoerr mounted brackets for orchids and staghorn ferns, which thrive in light that filters through a slat roof. LEFT: The vine clambering over the master-suite porch is yellow mandevilla (*Pentalinon luteum*).

The dining room overlooks—and hears—this gently bubbling water feature, OPPOSITE, built with the same stone used on nearby walls. Water lilies and papyrus inhabit the fountain, while dioon and elephant ear mix with ubiquitous ferns and philodendrons along the far side of the gravel. At right, twin pylons mark the base of the hillside staircase.

Island light and air permeate the living room, RIGHT, and other interiors designed by Tom Scheerer. A cozily upholstered banquette bridges an archway to join chairs, tables, tree trunks, and a turf rug in an indoor-outdoor sitting room. Buffed stone paving reflects the pavilion's lantern-like luminosity, as do branches softly uplighted against the night sky. The bromeliad *Alcantarea imperialis*, ensconced in a glamorous pot, gleams in the shadows.

The property's most eye-opening pavilion, OPPOSITE, stands aloof from the house, perched as it is on a hill farther inland. Hoerr conceived it as a belvedere with panoramic views out of range of the compound down below. This rustic lookout was built with greenheart, a famously durable, insect-resistant South American wood often used in the Caribbean.

The climb from the domestic landscape begins at this welcoming stairway, LEFT, perfectly aligned with the main axis through courtyard and living room. On either side, bougainvillea spills over retaining walls topped by native Caribbean 'Shady Lady' black olive trees (*Bucida buceras*). The head of the stairs connects to a path, ABOVE, that winds toward the lookout. Gazing back over clumps of plumbago and fragrant oleander, one can see the crowns of tall coconut palms near the house.

# 900 North Michigan Avenue

CHICAGO 2007–2011



An upmarket address with a downer of a view gives condominium shoppers pause for thought. Prospective buyers at this Gold Coast high-rise did not hesitate to pay top dollar for east-facing condos with coveted views of Lake Michigan. The developer worried, though, about tepid reactions to equally luxurious western units, because their windows stared inland across the bleak, gray 13,900-square-foot roof over lower stories in the mixed-use complex. Doug Hoerr flipped this liability into an asset in 2007 by concealing the roof under a well-appointed garden for residents to enjoy in common. "Even if they don't sit or have cookouts down there," Hoerr says, "they feel like it's their own private balcony." What they may not realize is that this is also their own piece of the prairie.

Believing that a garden should embody an expansive sense of place, and that Chicago is "the place where the prairie meets the lakefront," Hoerr looked westward from 900 North Michigan toward the Great Plains. His mind's eye saw the blocks of the city grid recede into the vast rectangles of farm fields, a pattern handed down by the Northwest Ordinance of 1787. That time-lapse rewind inspired the orthogonal geometry of Hoerr's green roof, as old-school as pioneer patchwork and as modern as a Mondrian abstraction at the nearby Art Institute.

Modular planting trays insulate the building below against seasonal temperature extremes, while absorbing storm runoff and ambient noise. "But I wanted everything to seem as if it just grew out of the ground—ground that happens to be ten stories off the street," Hoerr says. To strengthen that illusion, slabs of lightweight structural sheathing lift trays to the level of ipe-wood boardwalks and cast-stone entertainment decks. The plantings' prairie-meadow effect relies upon sedums, perennials, bulbs, self-seeding annuals "for randomness," and grasses that thrive at high altitude and refuse to collapse under snow. "Whenever the foliage catches the wind, you get the movement I always want to see in an urban environment," Hoerr adds. Varied plant heights add dimension and scale to the plantings, as do sociable pergolas and the vines climbing mesh enclosures that screen mechanical equipment.

Contrasting textures and colors carry the day on Hoerr's second rooftop, installed two years later over a parking garage in the same complex. Although accessible only for maintenance, these plantings form a collage on view to a host of neighboring structures. Vicarious appreciation, of course, goes only so far. Before long, Hoerr's client heard complaints from offices leasing two stories above a setback on the east side of the tower. "They were griping that *they* didn't have a green roof," Hoerr reports. The workplace amenity he created there in 2011 extrapolates the prairie aesthetic to a multilevel terrace with a cosmopolitan twist.

**Custom pergolas, OPPOSITE, give condo owners an intimate respite from looming skyscrapers. 'Karl Foerster' feather reed grass and *Verbena bonariensis* evoke prairie meadows. The residential West Terrace occupies the foreground of an aerial view, ABOVE, with eastern garage and office green roofs beyond.**

Modernist walkways and seating areas focus vistas on downtown skyscrapers and Lake Michigan as intently as any classical allée aligns with an obelisk or a Japanese pavilion frames a koi pond.

 A "before" photo, ABOVE, captures the glaring rooftop wasteland—bleak pavers, a little-used running track, and mechanical apparatus—that apartment windows originally surveyed. RIGHT: Architects Booth Hansen collaborated on the deck structure supporting the West Terrace's ecofriendly green roof tray system, as well as the design of pergolas framed with sustainably grown ipe wood.

Both of the 475-square-foot pergolas furnish shade and plenty of space where residents can relax and entertain. Flexible seating areas, BELOW RIGHT, face plantings of bulbs, annuals, and grasses whose flowers, foliage, and seed heads offer multiseasonal appeal. BELOW: Terrace floors juxtapose bluestone paving and ipe boardwalks in patterns attuned to the entire layout's strong rectangular geometry.

An office worker takes a break on the 6,900-square-foot East Terrace, TOP RIGHT, amid sedums, feather reed grass, and 'Millenium' alliums. Walks are oriented so that downtown landmarks like the pepper-pot-domed Old Water Tower terminate vistas as if they were garden follies.

The split-level grid of vegetation, MIDDLE RIGHT, was modeled on the pattern of Midwestern agricultural landscapes. Plantings also parallel the lake, appropriating it for an extraordinary urban horizon. BOTTOM RIGHT: Close to the set-back tower facade, wooden planters hold serviceberry trees, underplanted with cotoneaster, boxwood, and pachysandra, which act as a scrim to filter tenants' view of the terrace.

Although the 16,000-square-foot green roof over the parking garage, BOTTOM LEFT, is off-limits to visitors, its Mondrian-esque scheme of skylight and flora has become a well-loved public art piece for occupants of nearby buildings. Neighbors occasionally send Hoerr Schaudt thank-you notes for improving their property values as well as the scenery.

# McGovern Centennial Gardens

HERMANN PARK, HOUSTON 2014

 In 1942, Houston horticulturists welcomed the Garden Center, a new addition to Hermann Park, one of the city's largest public spaces created when a hometown oilman donated the site in 1914. Instead of the retail enterprise that its name implies today, the fifteen-acre Center initially consisted of specimen planting beds around a villa-like building where garden clubs could meet and stage exhibits; Later remodeling chipped away at the neoclassical architecture, a parking lot for the adjacent outdoor theater usurped much of the grounds, and sundry official gifts—from portrait busts to an orphaned Chinese pavilion—ended up here willy-nilly. Even after implementation of a 2005 master plan by Laurie Olin had rescued most of the 445-acre park from postwar decay, the Center remained, in Doug Hoerr's words, "a neglected, overpaved hodgepodge."

The pivotal location of the Center, between eminent cultural and medical complexes, galvanized the Hermann Park Conservancy to rethink this area's civic purpose, just as Olin had advised before bowing out, and to produce results in time for the approaching park centenary. When Hoerr Schaudt received the design commission in 2009—with James Patterson of White Oak Studio, landscape architect of record—the agenda included a vague desire for a structure for meetings and public events. But, Hoerr says, "It was thrilling that the Conservancy wanted us to do a master plan, and then help choose an architect. We could place the building where the garden needed it to be."

Although Hoerr razed the old Center headquarters to open up the core of the site, he honored Hermann Park's classical lineage with a grand symmetrical gesture: a 350-foot-long axial lawn flanked by symmetrical pergolas and varied series of thematic landscapes. These range from a formal Rose Garden to a rambling Woodland Walk, an Arid Garden stocked with dry-climate plants, and a Celebration Garden for weddings and other festivities. Hoerr Schaudt nestled the Chinese pavilion into an East Texas pine grove and organized a Sculpture Walk where Simón Bolívar now hobnobs happily with Robert Burns. Generations of families sharing a culinary heritage mingle amid the interactive Family Garden's vegetables, fruits, and herbs. "Houston is a big melting pot," Hoerr says, "and these gardens invite the city to experience different cultures through horticulture."

Architect Peter Bohlin of Bohlin Cywinski Jackson says, "From the very beginning, we were making a gateway—a calm building that responds to Doug's strong idea for the garden." The shimmering stainless-steel portal in Bohlin's stone-clad pavilion frames a dramatic vista of turf and water, previewing star attractions without giving the whole show away. Anticipation builds from the moment visitors pull

**The entrance through the Cherie Flores Garden Pavilion, OPPOSITE, narrows visitors' first view to an axial perspective of Centennial Green and the Mount. The Beaux-Arts-inspired layout of the landscape, ABOVE, nods to classical precedent elsewhere in historic Hermann Park, but its central vista also keeps contemporary Houston in the picture.**

into the transformed parking lot, now a lush grove of trees and grasses. Even out there, the proscenium-like entrance focuses all eyes on a gargantuan, conical mound at the far end of the greensward. This is technically a *mount*, an ornamental landscape feature dating back at least to the Renaissance. Hoerr gave his Texas update a gently sloped helical path, bisected by cascades. The platform at the summit, with panoramas linking Hermann Park to its urban environs, has attained must-see status for a constant stream of locals and tourists. It is the best place for surveying the animated landscape below and for plotting a jaunt into Houston garden central.

As wisteria steadily climbs the sturdy twin pergolas Hoerr Schaudt designed to flank the Green, LEFT, foliage and blossoms will sheathe their metallic gleam, creating verdant tunnels. OPPOSITE: Just outside these shady arbors, sunny borders overflow with a lavish mix of shrubs, perennials, and bulbs. The roll call includes bushy native, Southwestern yellow bells (*Tecoma stans*), drought-tolerant tuberous bulbine, Texan woolly stemodia (*Stemodia tomentosa*), tropical evergreen ixora, and humidity-loving calliandra. Horticultural consultant Johnny Steele Design advised on varieties best adapted to Houston's rigorous climate.

RESTROOMS

In a stunning aesthetic overlay, OPPOSITE, Peter Bohlin's sleek canopies frame Doug Hoerr's fanciful Mount as well as the no-nonsense late-twentieth-century concrete of the Houston Museum of Natural Science behind it. ABOVE RIGHT: The walk from parking lot to garden gateway focuses all eyes on the Mount, even before people cross the entrance pavilion threshold. RIGHT: The axis culminates in a rushing water feature that harks back to Italian Renaissance cascades. Hedges of dwarf yaupon holly (*Ilex vomitoria* 'Nana') edge the helical path between bands of zoysia grass.

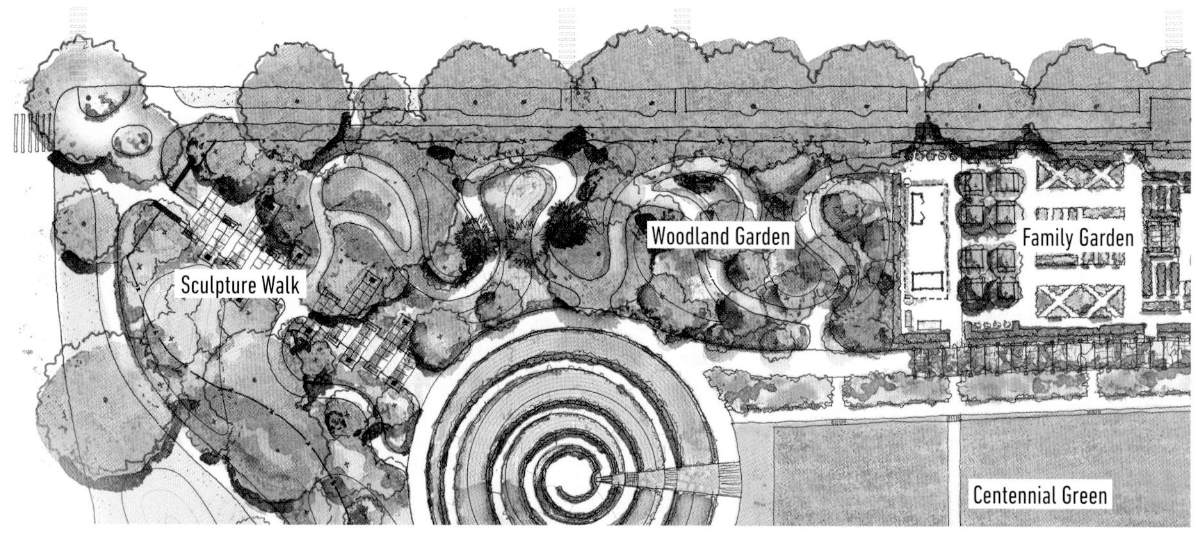
Woodland Garden
Family Garden
Sculpture Walk
Centennial Green

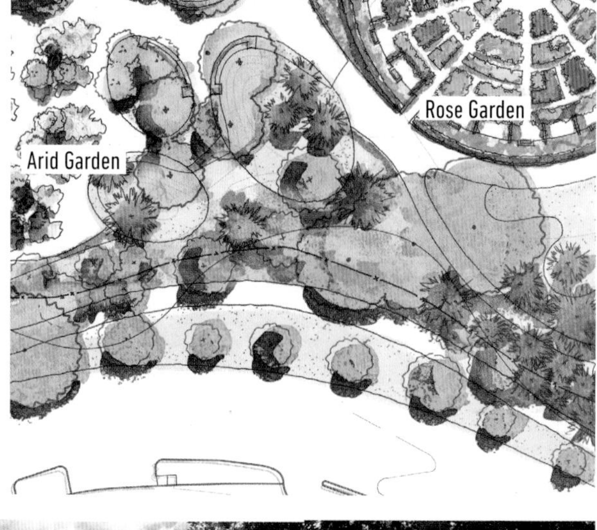
Rose Garden
Arid Garden

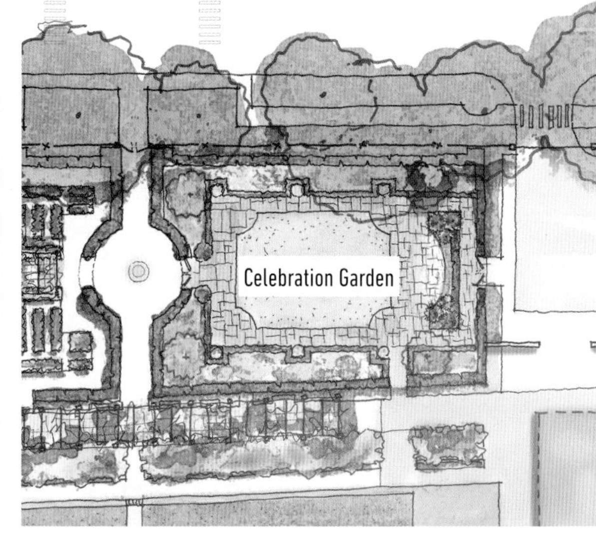
Celebration Garden

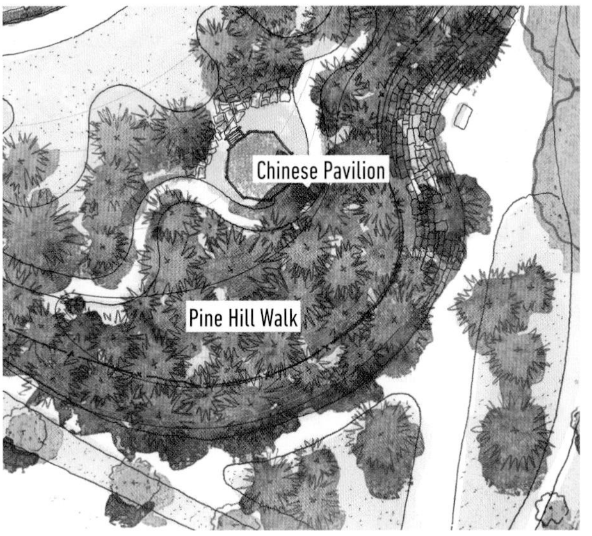
Chinese Pavilion
Pine Hill Walk

Even before exploring the Centennial Gardens proper, visitors leave their vehicles in a garden, OPPOSITE. The 294-car parking lot is generously planted with durable, drought-tolerant palo verde, Chinkapin oak (*Quercus muhlenbergii*), Mexican sycamore (*Platanus mexicana*), pink muhly grass (*Muhlenbergia capillaris*), and Berkeley sedge (*Carex divulsa*). Looking away from the Flores Pavilion, the oak allée aligns with a condominium tower.

Architecture, pool, and fountain jets, LEFT, channel a sideways vista over hedges and treetops to the Chinese Pavilion's golden "pagoda" roof. The dark, prowlike canopy of the Miller Outdoor Theatre, nearby in Hermann Park, joins the city skyline.

# Usher-Lambe Residence

PALM SPRINGS, CALIFORNIA 2015

Thanks to its desert locale and legendary trove of mid-20th-century butterfly roofs, breezeways, and boomerang pools, Palm Springs routinely gets tagged as a modernist "mecca." Likewise, many a vintage garden there suggests an "oasis" of putting-green turf, Technicolor flowers, and bottomless reservoirs dreamed up by some Rat Pack genie. A 1956 version of that magic lives on at the former estate of the Broadway and Hollywood composer Frederick Loewe (*My Fair Lady, Camelot, Gigi*), now a rental getaway and events venue owned by Chicago entrepreneurs Linda Usher and Malcolm Lambe. But when the couple decided to build a family vacation home on a lot next door—originally Loewe's three-hole golf course—they sought a 21st-century modern alternative to retro showmanship. Heavy-handed theatrics seemed impertinent amid terrain with its own haunting drama.

The luminous, finely honed planes of the new house by architect Laurence Booth, of Booth Hansen, almost levitate between the San Jacinto Mountains to the west and downtown Palm Springs farther east in the Coachella Valley. Space and panoramic views flow back and forth across thresholds, terraces, and an infinity pool, as well as through automatic sliding glass walls and an outdoor dining porch. Transparent surfaces that dissolve in shifting light also solidify to capture reflected palm trees and sunrises as ephemeral additions to Usher and Lambe's substantial art collection. Hoerr Schaudt expands upon this legerdemain in the landscape, disguising boundaries—and neighbors' houses—behind deftly graded berms and dense vegetation. The 1.6-acre property appears to stretch countless miles before meeting the valley's craggy rim.

Doug Hoerr took his cue from the stark splendor of desert and mountainside. Native boulders dominate the austere "moonscape" he designed to complement Booth's lapidary minimalism. Sinewy olive trees bring sculptural flamboyance to the front yard, alongside creeping rosemary, for evergreen color and texture, and bushy hedges of Indian fig laurel (*Ficus microcarpa nitida*) for privacy. Like the Texas sage (*Leucophyllum frutescens*), brittlebrush (*Encelia farinosa*), creosote bush (*Larrea tridentata*), oleander, and mesquite that screen the slope east of the house, these drought-tolerant plantings are sustainable with modest care in a region where annual rainfall averages 5.8 inches. Hoerr Schaudt replaced thirsty lawns with a continuous xeriscape of decomposed-granite. Fine enough to mimic drifts of desert sand, identical particles of weathered rock also cover the driveway (a glue-like stabilizer minimizes road dust), eliminating the line between pavement and ground. All along the approach to the entry, it looks as if boulders have fortuitously cleared a trail that materializes and vanishes like a mirage.

The front yard, BELOW, suggests a pristine stretch of windswept desert, its barely-there driveway fading into a rocky surround. Native boulders arranged with the knowing nonchalance of a Zen garden reinforce the natural effect, as if they had tumbled in from the San Jacinto Mountains behind the house. Olive trees and creeping rosemary give a settled air to the manmade ridge that screens neighbors. RIGHT: A thick evergreen hedge of Indian laurel fig ensures privacy without blocking the mountain backdrop to the west.

PREVIOUS PAGES: Architectural planes bracket the view eastward across the Coachella Valley. Tufts of yellow-flowered brittlebrush and pink muhly grass relieve the monochromatic poolside “moonscape.”

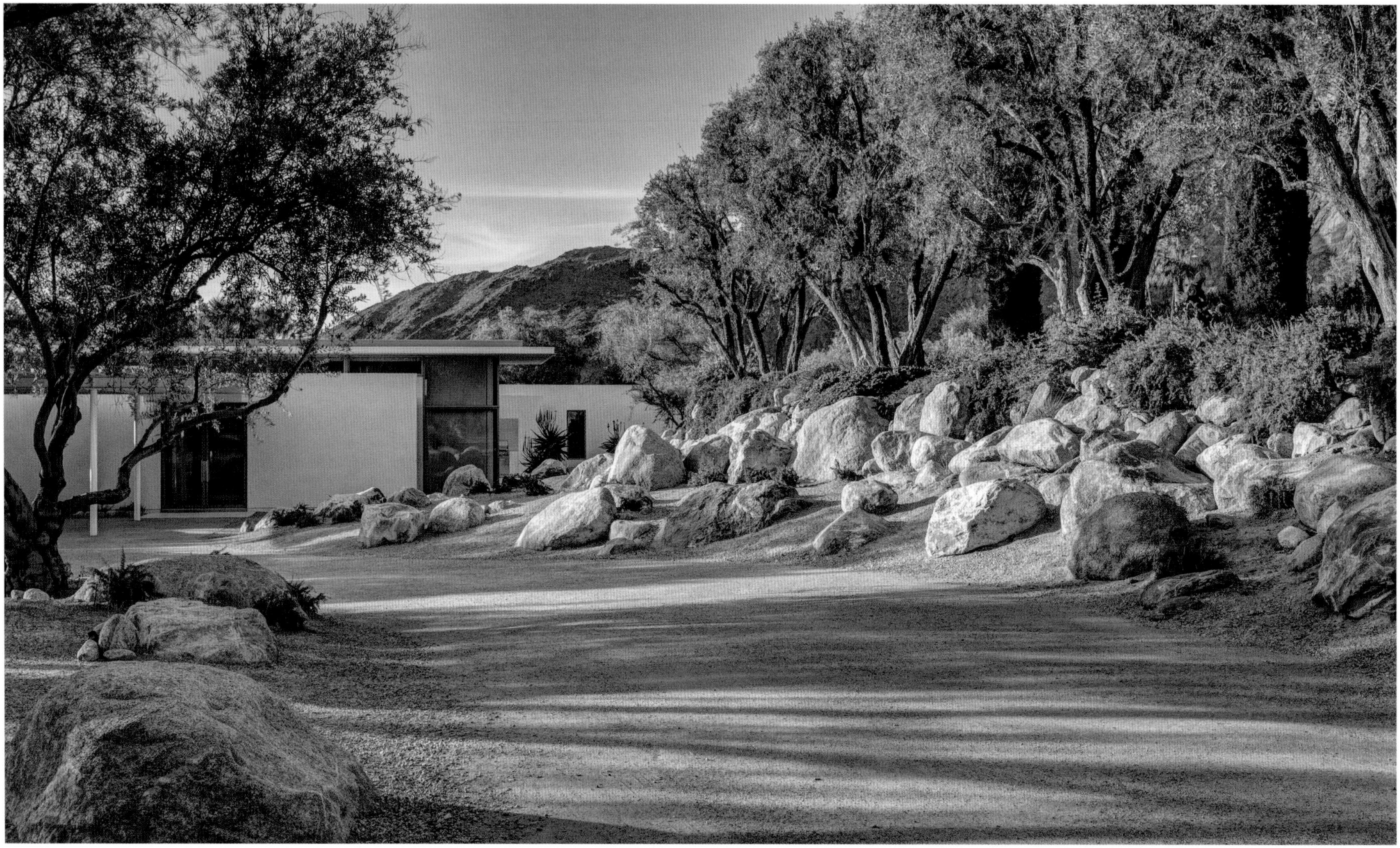

Rockwork crafted to resemble primeval formations, ABOVE, emphasizes the minimalist precision of Laurence Booth's take on midcentury California modernism. The living room's thin-profile windows (9-foot-square panels custom-built to glide open and shut on ball bearings) overlook craggy ledges where ornamental grass appears to have set seed by happenstance. In fact, each clump of fountain grass has been transplanted to a pocket expressly made for it.

By design, the enormous sheets of glass mirror the choreography of boulders and vegetation in the gravel-mulched xeriscape outside. LEFT: Outside the rear media room, a gnarled specimen olive tree partners with tall spiky Cape aloes (*Aloe ferox*), a succulent native to semi-arid regions of South Africa.

# Cascade House

CHICAGO'S NORTH SHORE 2010



When a prime lakefront homesite such as this boasts enviable views from a high bluff and the owners' program includes lots of elbow room for their three young sons, indoor and outdoor swimming pools, a gym, offices for both parents, guest rooms, and service quarters, "You could build a palace, like everybody does," says architect Peter Gluck. "We did the opposite. We built a big house that you hardly see, because it's embedded in the land." His reticent design is also forthrightly modern, as the clients wished, in contrast to their neighborhood's traditional norm. Gluck speaks matter-of-factly about "mining" the bluff's steep forty-two-foot eastern face to bury the bulk of a multilevel structure that steps down, or "cascades," toward the shore. At the front of the house, to the west, only a two-story glass pavilion rises above the precipice. But at the terraced back, generous living spaces on four levels command vistas of Lake Michigan.

Not a trace remains of the colossal dig, boulder revetment, and backfill that temporarily left the grounds looking as if an inland tsunami had struck. Melding his industry with Gluck's, Doug Hoerr rewrote topographic history to create the illusion of virgin terrain through which architectural planes

**Before "unfolding" layer by layer on its impressively steep descent to Lake Michigan, OPPOSITE, the house presents a reticent front to anyone nearing the inland entry, RIGHT, atop the bluff. Quaking aspens' white bark and glossy leaves partially screen windows that allow just a peek at the watery horizon.**

Another teaser for the lake, BELOW, winks through a reclaimed-wood fence that shields the family terrace from the entrance court. Raised beds overflow with liriope, 'Big Daddy' hosta, and ostrich fern beneath a Kentucky coffee tree and climbing Hydrangea anomala ssp. petiolaris. Dense greenery intensifies the sense of hidden surprises yet to be unveiled. ABOVE: Over the fence, more hydrangea spreads a tapestry behind the family terrace's alfresco dining table.

and volumes had emerged like natural outcrops of crystalline bedrock. He channeled fluid landforms and vegetation around and over the building's angular tectonic shifts to fuse interiors with rooftop terraces, ramps, stairs, and, ultimately, the shore. "It's a continuous sensation of unfolding," Hoerr says. On his advice, a freestanding boathouse initially planned for the northern end of the beach was tucked under the outdoor pool, leaving a seamless swath of green shoreline to be enjoyed from above.

With the main residence hugging the property's eastern rim, most of the three-acre rectangular plateau stretches westward to the public street. Here too the owners wished to blaze a stylistic trail away from the tonsorial boxwoods and manicured lawns of suburbs like theirs. Hoerr began by winding a 450-foot driveway through naturalistic plantings. Their density buffers privacy, softens boundary lines, and fuels suspense. Instead of approaching the house head-on, Gluck says, "You sneak up on what seems like a very small glass structure—and then you see right through it." On the open landscape that descends beyond the entry, Hoerr massed bayberry, rugosa roses, Sargent juniper, dune grass, and other flora tough enough to survive winters on the lake. He also craned in more than a dozen large trees over the top of the house to add a crucial layer of visual unfolding. "Doug understands that, after the first blast of a view like this, it can turn into a picture," Gluck says. "Ten minutes later, you don't see the picture anymore. But when you look at the view through a foreground of tall trees, it's dynamic. Your experience only multiplies."

**Two stories down from the front door, RIGHT, the pool terrace's redbud trees and honey locusts, mugo pines and daylilies establish a domestic-scaled foreground to the vast lake while easing angular bluestone into undulant terrain. All trees were individually selected for their "non-nursery" shapes.**

The same bluestone that paves the lower terrace, OPPOSITE, also lines the indoor pool, behind the glass wall. Interiors by Anne Kaplan, of Insight Environmental Design, reflect the firm's intensive collaboration with Hoerr Schaudt, Peter Gluck, and their clients. THIS PAGE, CLOCKWISE FROM ABOVE: Alongside an outdoor staircase, a swath of evergreen wintercreeper (*Euonymous fortunei* 'Coloatus') lets the hillside flow, unbroken, through a rift in the house. Stepping-stones mount the turfed green roof that gently slopes above the indoor pool. That incline levels off—and the ratio of paving to grass increases—at a hospitable lookout terrace accessible from major indoor entertaining spaces.

# Bissell Residence

GRAND RAPIDS, MICHIGAN 2009

Behind a filigree of eastern redbud in flower, OPPOSITE, flights of stairs and landings zigzag down the precipitous hillside to Reeds Lake. ABOVE: Oak, shagbark hickory, sugar maple, and linden spread a woodland canopy above the dockside guest cottage. Like the main house, this was designed by Rugo/Raff.

The Prairie Style romance that now defines this property started out in need of a matchmaker. Mark and Cathy Bissell's contemporary residence on the crest of a knoll, designed by Steve Rugo of Rugo/Raff Architects, had just the right low-slung ease to pair with the rural lake below—except that a forty-foot drop separated house from shore. Hoerr Schaudt advised that access to the water, however desirable it might be, should wait until the building itself had acquired visible means of support. Physical reinforcement was essential because ground fell away sharply from the foundation on all sides and construction had denuded some nearby woodland, increasing the risk of erosion.

Aesthetics mattered too, because, Doug Hoerr explains, "We didn't want the house to look propped up." Its horizontal profile and rugged masonry inspired his low retaining walls of the same Colorado moss rock, which unobtrusively extend architecture into irregular terrain. These sandstone-capped enclosures ramble to accommodate shifts in elevation as well as the mature trees, new plantings, and pools that visually link terraces for outdoor living to the cultivated wilderness all around.

Similar concerns persuaded Hoerr to avoid the obvious solution to the Bissells' lakefront slope: a single straight staircase. "I stood on the shore," he says, "and I thought, 'Look at the lines of that house. Instead of a vertical slash, don't you want to have a zigzag of landings and steps that goes down, down, down—parallel to those roofs—with rhythms that make the whole thing an *event*?'"

His concept translated into three staggered flights of stairs perpendicular to the upper terraces and connected by three broad landings, which appear to hover beside the knoll. As detailed by Rugo/Raff, taut wires strung through aluminum railing posts repeat the horizontals of the steps; the steel-framed landings are cantilevered off the hillside—and engineered to reduce their structural impact. Hoerr notes that, "Breaking up the stairs encourages people to pause and enjoy the view, listen to water falling off the zero-edge swimming pool, or maybe catch their breath."

The staircase carefully bypasses existing redbud trees, which Hoerr Schaudt released from invasive species that had hogged the understory canopied by oak, shagbark hickory, sugar maple, and linden. Redbud branches, blossoms, and foliage weave a lacy, year-round screen for excursions uphill and down. A path at the base of the stairs leads to a stone fire circle, a curved play lawn, and a cozy lakeside guesthouse. From spring into fall, daffodils, Spanish bluebells, astilbe, daylilies, eupatorium, and asters take turns brightening strolls to water's edge. Panicgrass and goldenrod join native shrubs and trees in filtering out neighbors' docks—one less distraction during rendezvous with great blue herons and trumpeter swans.

In the entry courtyard, LEFT, a Scots pine's lower branches reiterate the horizontality of broad eaves and continuous windows, which anchor the house to the brow of a knoll. With similar intent, and using identical Colorado moss rock and limestone, Hoerr Schaudt staggered a parallel series of low walls through the court, BELOW. Their right angles are softened by a meadowlike groundcover of spreading lily turf (*Liriope spicata*) and long-blooming 'Summer Beauty' allium.

Custom-designed limestone containers attuned to the building's lines, LEFT, are planted for multiseasonal texture and color. This spring show features bleeding heart, columbine, and viola. BELOW LEFT: Doug Hoerr recycled water from a pool at the side of the house into a fountain that drowns out noisy utility equipment. BELOW: Stairs from the entry level to the lower story, notched into the hill, deploy architectural geometry to frame vegetation. The ample foliage of multistem redbud and oakleaf hydrangea contrasts with dense carpets of myrtle (*Vinca minor*).

Consistency in materials throughout the site reinforces spatial links. The French limestone on the pool deck, OPPOSITE, also paves the living room floor, just inside. With its infinity edge, the swimming pool visually extends the terrace to the lake forty feet below, while hillside stairs, RIGHT, draw a sight line to the guest cottage. BELOW: Hoerr relieved the precipitous climb by breaking the staircase into flights of steps between cantilevered landings, as shown in cross-section, BELOW RIGHT.

A two-track stone-and-concrete drive lined by maples, LEFT, curves downhill to water's edge for boat access. Daffodils bloom amid roadside *Epimedium* x *versicolor* 'Sulphureum' and myrtle. The fire circle beside the play lawn, ABOVE, is another lakefront destination. Plants on the floodplain at the base of the knoll are predominantly natives that can tolerate yearly submersion.

One fork of the main drive, ABOVE, leads to the front door while the other bends downhill past a weeping katsura tree and rhododendrons toward the garage tucked under the entry court garden. Cotoneaster trails above the garage doors. LEFT: The masonry used throughout the project makes its first appearance in walls along the public road. The sinuous bars of a custom steel gate conjure up forest shadows as well as rippling water and campfire smoke.

# Trump International Hotel and Tower

CHICAGO 2009



In the name of progress, Chicagoans have been tinkering with the Chicago River since the early 1800s: diverting its flow into canals, rerouting its course for navigation and industry, spanning it with more than sixty drawbridges, reversing the direction of its current, dyeing it green for St. Patrick's Day, and from 2001 on transforming a nine-block stretch of its downtown south bank into a public esplanade, the Riverwalk. The waterway can almost seem like an artifact—except when a flood reasserts its primal force. Peter Schaudt addressed this split personality in landscapes for the plaza at Trump Tower, a ninety-two-story hotel/condominium that opened in 2009 along one of the Riverwalk's busiest segments.

The plaza descends from street level to the waterside walkway in three tiers, with the largest area up top, outside the skyscraper entry. "We offset the architecture's cool, hard gloss by infusing natural textures and colors," Schaudt said. "Our design abstracts what you'd find growing on 'unimproved' Illinois riverbanks. It's an homage to the Trump site's original ecology." Schaudt accomplished his riparian retrospective most fully on the highest terrace, planting 16,000 square feet of native species and other regionally appropriate plants in the horticultural palette he assembled with help from principal John Evans. Alders, bottlebrush buckeye, Joe-pye weed, prairie grasses, serviceberry, sumac, and the like qualified this four-season display as downtown Chicago's first landscape designed using indigenous flora at a major commercial development.

Its creator pragmatically employed extensive containers to raise plants several feet above human ear level as noise baffles. The dense trees, shrubs, and prairie grasses that lured native birds also blocked out urban eyesores. Schaudt relished the formidable sleight of hand that few visitors would notice consciously. A cross-section drawing lays bare the "natural" riverbank's substratum of transportation tunnels, below-grade shops, and utilities. The plaza is in fact an enormous green roof with five independent structural systems. Resulting variations in load-bearing capacity obliged the design team to calculate minute shifts in weight, altering soil composition and depth from planter to planter, even within single containers. To passersby, though, the finished installation appeared firmly rooted, utterly consistent.

In November 2010, Mayor Daley's Landscape Awards Program declared the new plaza a civic treasure, "a poetic interpretation of native Illinois that seems at once sophisticated and familiar." Alas, this familiarity lasted only six months. One day in May 2011, Schaudt said, "Somebody came to our office door and yelled, 'Hey, Peter, they're ripping out your native stuff at Trump! What's going on?' I had no clue." He soon learned that the Trump Organization had already hired another Chicago landscape architect to clear everything but the soil and trees, and replace allegedly unkempt natives with a tidy high-low carpet of evergreens, annuals, and gravel strips fit for a suburban mall. Schaudt posted an elegy on The Shouting Hare blog that June: "Landscape architecture is by nature ephemeral. As designers, we plan for ... the moment of installation as well as the changes that will occur as living things reach maturity ... I deeply appreciated the opportunity to create a meaningful space that touched the emotions of so many."

**The glass-and-stainless-steel skin of Skidmore, Owings & Merrill's riverside tower, OPPOSITE, sets off the warmth of mums and fountain grass in a lobby-level fall planting. Cascading 'Silver Falls' dichondra reflects both metallic and aqueous tones while boxwoods pick up green trim on the terra-cotta-clad Wrigley Building, a 1923 skyscraper at the plaza's upstream (eastern) end, ABOVE.**

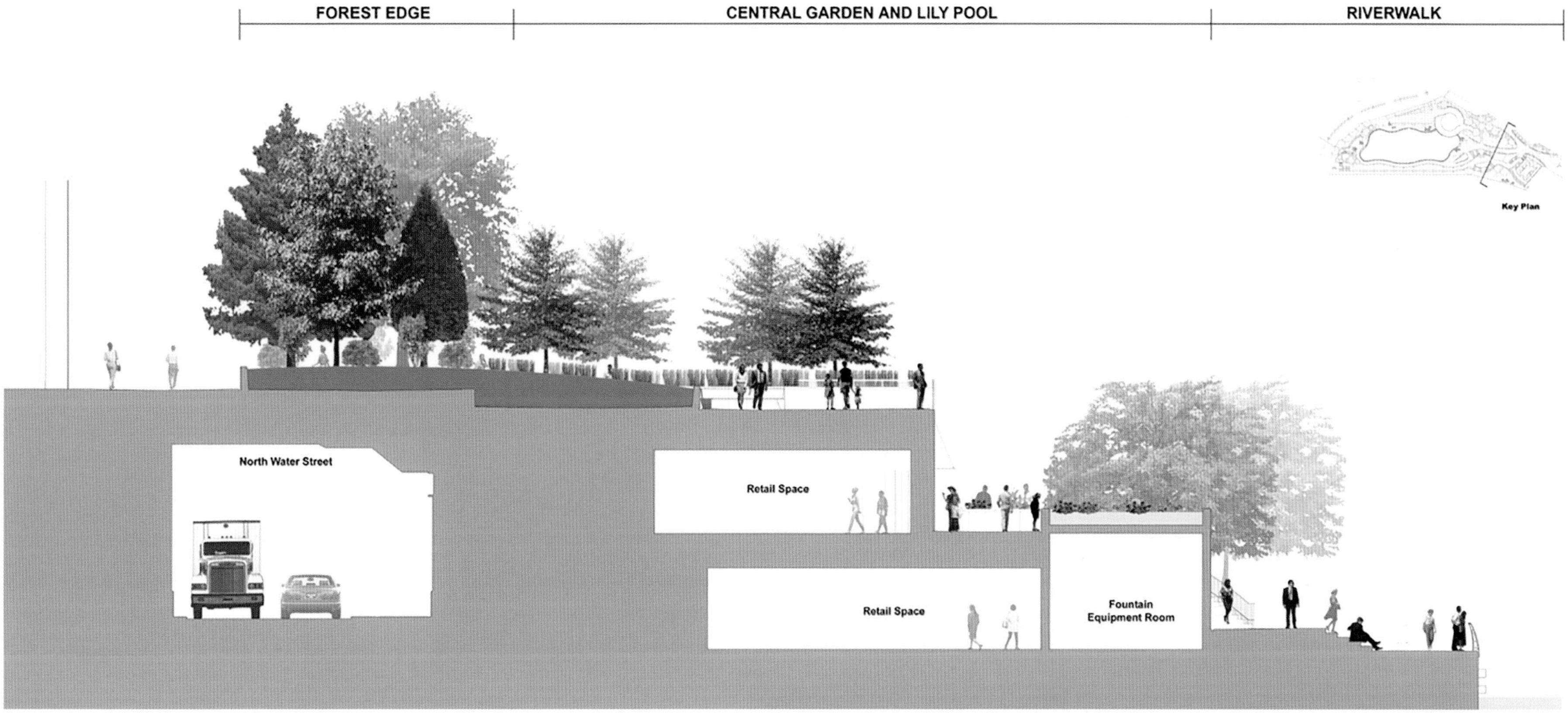

FOREST EDGE | CENTRAL GARDEN AND LILY POOL | RIVERWALK

Key Plan

North Water Street

Retail Space

Retail Space

Fountain
Equipment Room

Riparian habitat meets high-rise, OPPOSITE, as the autumn foliage of cut-leaf staghorn sumac (*Rhus typhina* 'Laciniata') blazes above bright green horsetail (*Equisetum*), red-berried cotoneaster, and pale plumes of *Miscanthus sinensis* 'Nippon.' Swiss stone pine (*Pinus cembra*) contributes height and structure to this urban "forest edge" tableau. A cross-section through subterranean infrastructure and amenities stepping down to the public Riverwalk, ABOVE, exposes the wizardry of Peter Schaudt's naturalistic scheme. RIGHT: Acoustic insulation from plantings raised above human ear level helps pedestrians to concentrate on chirping birds, not honking horns.

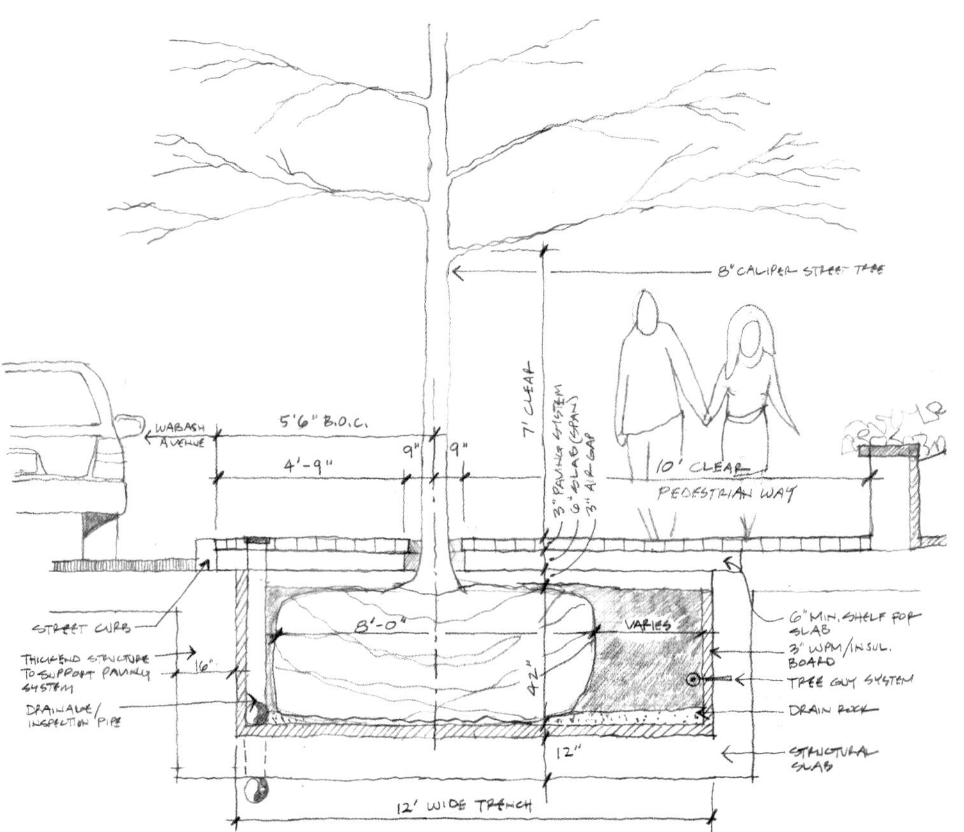
8" CALIPER STREET TREE
WABASH AVENUE
5'6" B.O.C.
9"
9"
4'-9"
7' CLEAR
3" PAVING SYSTEM
6" SLAB (SPAN)
3" AIR GAP
10' CLEAR
PEDESTRIAN WAY
STREET CURB
THICKENED STRUCTURE TO SUPPORT PAVING SYSTEM
DRAINAGE/INSPECTION PIPE
16"
8'-0"
VARIES
42"
6" MIN. SHELF FOR SLAB
3" WPM/INSUL. BOARD
TREE GUY SYSTEM
DRAIN ROCK
12"
STRUCTURAL SLAB
12' WIDE TRENCH

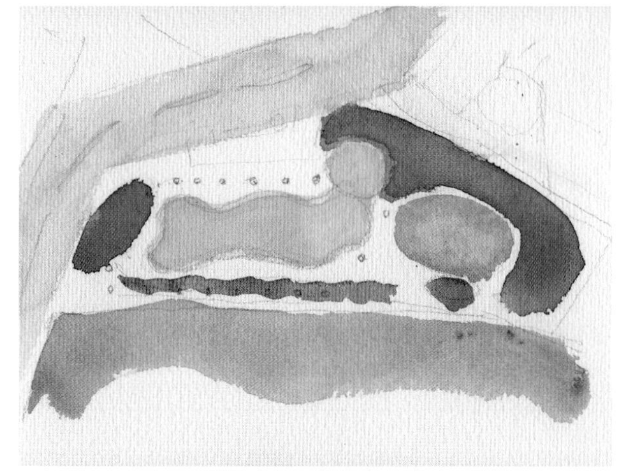

Even on the plaza's most densely planted tier, LEFT, trees, shrubs, and tall grasses frame inviting views of the Chicago River to the south, with more than a century of "modern improvements" on full display. A pyramidal 'Whitespire Senior' gray birch salutes the landmark Michigan Avenue drawbridge and taller neighbors.

OPPOSITE, CLOCKWISE FROM TOP RIGHT: In an early watercolor conceptual site plan, Schaudt roughed out basic relationships between water, architecture, and vegetation, whether ostensibly earthbound and hardy (green), or frankly containerized and transient (orange). Virtually everything, however, grows in some sort of container atop an engineered base, from street trees along Wabash Avenue (on the plaza's northern side) to prairie groves in Trump Tower's heartland, to a formal bosque of shade trees at the Riverwalk terminus.

# Greater Des Moines Botanical Garden

DES MOINES, IOWA 2015



Right on trend for 1979, the newly opened Des Moines Botanical Center decided to house its core plant collection beneath a geodesic dome. During the next quarter-century, though, funds dried up, displays languished under the leaky Plexiglas lid, meager outdoor beds fell into disrepair, and attendance slowed to a trickle. Even casual drop-ins who would have settled for a safe, quiet patch of greenery found no reason to return. On one side, Interstate 235 roared incessantly; straight ahead, a double-lane parkway cut through the grounds, slicing off frontage on the Des Moines River. "If you didn't get hit by a car," says Doug Hoerr, "you could cross to the riverbank and see the downtown skyline. This city exists because two rivers converge here—in an agricultural region that's all about water—and yet the Center turned its back on the river."

**The Water Garden, OPPOSITE, looks like an offshoot of the outlying river where giant waterlilies (*Victoria amazonica*), cannas, and pickerelweed happen to have berthed near the boardwalk. Onshore, boxwood globes mediate between lilypad discs and the Conservatory dome, ABOVE, a visitor's center and exhibition space.**

He voiced his candid observations in 2004, upon joining an energetic design committee of board members, donors, and horticultural-society volunteers. Their goal was to expand and elevate what would soon be called the Greater Des Moines Botanical Garden into a first-class civic institution on a par with the city's celebrated museums and opera. The unsung genius of the garden, Hoerr concluded, was water. Tapping its potential in a new master plan yielded fresh opportunities to engage the public in horticulture, ecology, and history. "It's fine, of course, to teach about runoff, nitrates, and bioswales," Hoerr says, "though you can't forget that people come here for beauty, to immerse themselves in nature, and maybe give the kids a wild moment with water."

Although rerouting the parkway cleared a swath of riverside, logistical concerns still limited pedestrian access to the bank. "Then it struck me," Hoerr recalls. "Why not bring the river up to the foreground, right next to the dome?" Groovy again, this Space Age period piece was refurbished as a conservatory and entrance pavilion, a transitional zone where visitors get up close and personal with extraordinary flora—"Exotics that don't normally grow in Iowa," says director of horticulture Kelly Norris–before venturing into the garden proper.

At the far end of the conservatory, doors open to a café terrace and a boardwalk that seems to float above a half-acre body of water. Hoerr contrived the vista so that the surface of his Water Garden pool appears to merge with the river. "That view pulls you out of the conservatory," says Stephanie Jutila, the garden's president and CEO. "The brilliance of Hoerr Schaudt's designs for this whole landscape is that each experience releases you into another." The boardwalk angles sideways, unmistakably aligning

with an on-shore allée, which in turn leads to destinations alive with innovative ideas that Iowans can try at home. "We think of ourselves as a living museum of modern horticulture," Norris adds. "This place reflects the horticulture of our time. It's not a static reference to a single past era, and how people thought about gardening then. We want the landscape to be in constant motion."

But before moving on to see subalpine vegetation in the Conifer and Gravel Garden, or prairie ecotypes in the Hillside Garden, visitors often linger in the Water Garden. They lean over the railings for a better look at Japanese water iris and pickerelweed, as the plash of a cascade along the terrace rim muffles the din from I-235. "Crossing that acoustic threshold," Jutila says, "people are transported in time and place." More than 300,000 people, in fact, took that journey during the reinvented Des Moines Botanical Garden's first season, a 53 percent jump over 2013 that confirmed the escalating value of liquid assets.

This waterfall cantilevers off the Hillside Garden, on a natural rise east of the riverbank, and pours into a pool beside the elliptical Celebration Lawn. Jutting well above the pool rim, RIGHT, the concrete spout gives visitors a behind-the-scenes experience of hydraulic drama. To the south, the Conservatory's 80-foot-tall geodesic dome looms above shrubby native serviceberry trees (*Amelanchier x grandiflora*), a favorite food source for birds, which now grace perennial borders of allium, nepeta, and penstemon.

Expanding upon the principles of his English mentor Beth Chatto, a dry-garden pioneer, Doug Hoerr designed the Dorothy and Max Rutledge Conifer Garden, OPPOSITE, as a gravel-mulched showcase for 250 species of xeric, subalpine, and steppe perennials, shrubs, and, of course, notable conifers. Standouts in the curved beds include *Pinus* 'Hillside Creeper,' *Thuja* 'Gold Drop,' *Chamaecyparis nootkatensis* 'Green Arrow,' and *Larix decidua* 'Pendula.'

State Street maples (*Acer miyabei* 'Morton') line the 220-foot long Ruan Allée, LEFT. The architectural spine of Hoerr's master plan, this symmetrical promenade honors John Ruan III and Janis Ruan, leaders in the public beautification of Des Moines. Reclaimed bricks edging the pavement were made at a factory that occupied the Botanical Garden property in the early twentieth century.

Meandering beside a perimeter fence between the Water Garden and the river, the eco-savvy Lauridsen Savanna, BELOW LEFT, combines oaks, alders, and other deciduous trees from temperate regions with a matrix of sedges and grasses. Added seasonal color comes from bulbs and perennials like amsonia, aster, camassia, eupatorium, helenium, iris, and lobelia.

Befitting its role as a popular venue for performances, weddings, and other festive events, the Celebration Lawn in the Koehn Garden, BELOW RIGHT, has a grand symmetrical enclosure. The waterfall, on axis with the main entrance off the Ruan Allée, is a prime background for bridal ceremonies. ABOVE RIGHT: Wide borders reinterpret Edwardian herbaceous opulence for the Midwest, mixing classic perennials such as catmint, coreopsis, daylily, lamb's ear, phlox, and salvia with grasses, annuals, and bulbs. At the Koehn Garden's northwest corner, OPPOSITE, a gateway opens onto seven acres ripe for future Botanical Garden expansion. A vine and gourd exhibit, a meadow and wildflower area, a plot for edibles and family projects, and a native Iowa woodland garden are some of the possibilities under consideration.

The Water Garden boardwalk conducts visitors to the start of the Allée, OPPOSITE. A foliage-framed westward vista over the yew hedge takes in urns on the Belvedere—a formal esplanade overlooking the river—and an arch of the University Avenue Bridge. RIGHT: Clipped boxwood edges one of the Belvedere's two parterres, where Kelly Norris and his team annually rotate plantings flamboyant enough to hold their own against the downtown Des Moines skyline. ABOVE: Water Garden cascades dampen the roar of a nearby interstate. ABOVE RIGHT: Canna, lotus, and hydrangea light up the intersection of the boardwalk with a café terrace outside the Conservatory.

# Renker Garden

HARBOR SPRINGS, MICHIGAN 2012

Roaring Brook rushes through a cultivated woodland of cedar, hemlock, and rhododendron, OPPOSITE. The third in a series of four custom cedar footbridges leads to the 1,800-square-foot cottage. Just beyond the fourth crossing, ABOVE, the stream empties into Little Traverse Bay.



Generations of high achievers have learned to go with the flow on Roaring Brook. An 1898 guide to Michigan resorts praised this "romping stream of crystal purity, having its rise in numberless springs...and winding its way through...thick cedars, birches and hemlocks until at last tumbling over its rocky bed it pours itself into [Little Traverse Bay]." Those words still ring true on the two-acre property where brook meets bay. Greg and Stacey Renker purchased this spot as a rustic escape, barely two miles, or a five-minute sailboat ride, from the elegant summer compound they share with their three sons and many guests.

Greg has happy memories of Roaring Brook from boyhood, when he idled on a beach at the stream mouth and wondered what lay hidden within the strictly private greenery above it. When he and Stacey first entered his dreamworld as adults, they found that even though the parcel had eluded development, a prior owner had cleared large areas of native vegetation. Instead of winding through beautiful native flora, as it did in a forest preserve upstream, the brook passed lanky rhododendrons and bland lawns. Doug Hoerr, a lifelong summer regular in these parts, promised to create a woodland, artful yet wild, where Roaring Brook could romp again and the Renkers could rough it in style.

Skillful insertion of the same tree species cited in the old guidebook framed the armature for a suitably fluid plan. Sinuous walkways hint at secret destinations like the paths on a storybook treasure map. Each route eventually crosses one of the four footbridges that Hoerr built over the brook. "We made sure everybody goes over the water as often as possible, watches it catch the light, and listens," he says. Back on solid ground, a luxuriant understory of mainly native perennials eddies and swells under the sylvan canopy. Unfazed by demanding shade conditions and wet soils, Hoerr and associate principal Steve Gierke timed horticultural spectacles to coincide with the Renkers' visits in June through August. "We arranged plants in drifts like those in the woods," Gierke says, "so there's always a burst of color somewhere." Greens and blues predominate on a grassy terrace facing the bay, one of several spots left open to accommodate family play and entertaining.

One can imagine fairytale forest-dwellers hosting garden parties at the cottage that Katherine Hillbrand of SALA Architects designed "to appear as if it grew out of the earth." The same local master builders who crafted Hillbrand's undulating roof and primordial-looking boulder walls also fashioned Hoerr's stone wellhead for an artesian spring, which he channeled into a graceful serpentine rill. If the house recalls quirky mid-twentieth-century landmarks by Michigan architect Earl Young, the rill harks back to a Georgian locus classicus by the English landscape pioneer William Kent. Ripples in time at Roaring Brook hold particularly poignant meaning for Greg Renker. "Because the garden Doug made is remarkably ever-changing," he says, "it's a reminder to live in the moment. Any day that we miss seeing this place will never come again."

In a vein of fanciful rusticity dear to Northern Michigan, OPPOSITE, Katherine Hillbrand of SALA Architects used gargantuan native stones and generous eaves to create a grand-yet-cozy exterior fireplace. Hoerr Schaudt provided a hearthside terrace of compatible scale, overflowing its chiseled edges with an abundance of heuchera, hosta, ostrich fern, and rodgersia. This shapely foliage segues into a wilder blur of sedge, vernonia, solidago, and eupatorium as it nears the woods.

A rock-lined rill slices through a lawn's flawless carpet, ABOVE LEFT, in a contrast of figure and ground. Pattern and texture are also layered with color in wandering path borders, ABOVE RIGHT. White alyssum creeps onto flagstone, and yellow daylilies bend above purple gay feather (*Liatris*) spikes.

1 First Bridge
2 Roaring Brook
3 Second Bridge
4 Artesian Wellhead
5 Third Bridge
6 Private Beach Cove
7 Fourth Bridge
8 Rill

Each of the bridges is a site-specific design, crafted with the same attention to detail as outdoor furniture. The clean geometry of the first bridge, OPPOSITE, presents a simple foil to rugged tree trunks, a fine-leaved groundcover of myrtle and sweet woodruff, and whimsical stone toadstools that the Renkers' interior designer, Tom Stringer, found in France. Doug Hoerr keyed the rustic stickwork of the second bridge's railings, LEFT, to its luxuriant sylvan setting. Garnished with hostas, ferns, and variegated Solomon's seal, the timber deck interlocks precisely with the irregular profile of flagstones on the connecting path.

Along a woodland walk from the cottage to the second bridge, OPPOSITE, vertical strokes of 'Whitespire' birch, a horizontal green web of Irish moss (*Sagina subulata*) between flagstones, and blue drifts of Siberian bugloss (*Brunnera macrophylla*) lead the way. RIGHT: A picturesque wellhead displays the craftsmanship of Harbor Springs contractor Jeff Ford, whose firm, Evening Star Joinery, built all of the landscape structures here as well as the cottage. Water from this font spills into a pebble-lined rill, ABOVE RIGHT, which eventually flows to the lake. A beardtongue with wine-red foliage (*Penstemon* 'Dark Towers') underscores the glow of golden coneflowers (*Rudbeckia hirta*). ABOVE LEFT: Standing almost four feet tall at maturity, eye-popping *Astilboides tabularis* spreads its ruffled leaves over a grassy thicket of glaucous sedge (*Carex flacca* 'Blue Zinger').

# Botany Pond University of Chicago

CHICAGO 2004

In *Plant Relations: A First Book of Botany*, published in 1899, John Merle Coulter (1851–1928) wrote, "The study of plant societies, to determine their conditions of living, is one of the chief purposes of botanical field work." Three years later Professor Coulter, first chairman of the University of Chicago Department of Botany, advised landscape architects John C. Olmsted and Frederick Law Olmsted Jr. on plans for a pond within the university's recently built Hull Court Biology Quadrangle.

Like many Olmsted designs, this water feature combined formal edges with naturalistic vegetation. Coulter chose individual plants, both terrestrial and aquatic, for his pocket ecosystem according to their applicability as teaching and research material. Students soon instituted extracurricular uses for Botany Pond, as it came to be known. Freshmen who dared to forego their class's identifying green cap were subject to a spring dunking. So were losers in the senior moustache-growing "race" and participants in the annual intramural tug-of-war waged from opposite banks. Romantics still swear that couples who kiss on the Class of 1922 bridge are sure to marry.

Aside from some indomitable ginkgo trees, the Coulter-era planting scheme was barely a memory when Doug Hoerr began to restore the pond almost a century after its début. His thriving plant society does the professor proud in its taxonomic and seasonal diversity, while it burnishes the Olmsted legacy with an adventurous range of texture, scale, and color. Many current plant varieties represent innovations that have greatly expanded the palette available to turn-of-the-twentieth-century gardeners, such as winter-blooming *Hamamelis* x *intermedia* 'Arnold Promise,' a witch hazel first grown from seed at Harvard the year of Coulter's death but introduced to commerce only in 1963; the crab apple *Malus sargentii* 'Candymint,' which has red-rimmed pink flowers, patented in 1989; and the Japanese forest grass *Hakonechloa macra* 'Aureola,' a novel import to the United States during the 1990s. Coulter, like his contemporary Claude Monet, would delight in the present crop of water lilies.

*Postscript: A current University of Chicago guide to dorms reports that the namesake of Coulter House "is memorialized today by a small plastic rhododendron on the second-floor stairwell."*

Water lilies preside in the pond, OPPOSITE, for a botanical convocation on terra firma that hosts *Lysimachia punctata* 'Alexander,' *Calamagrostis brachytricha*, *Alchemilla mollis*, a weeping *Acer palmatum*, *Tradescantia* 'Concord Grape,' and, BELOW, bronzy *Ligularia dentata* 'Britt Marie Crawford' with a duck. ABOVE: Intramural sport makes a splash in 1957.

Extreme weather and acts of God can transform a landscape overnight. Biology imposes its own dynamic. And then there's human nature. "Change is key to our design mentality," says Doug Hoerr. "But knowing that people are ephemeral too, we'll plant a mature oak, not a sapling, so clients can enjoy it during their lifetime. Don't blame Millennials. Centuries earlier, Le Nôtre and Capability Brown did the same thing." Adaptability guided by historical perspective informs some of Hoerr Schaudt's most distinctive work, even when the site already bears the mark of an Olmsted, a Jensen, or other master. Balancing heritage with modernity poses formidable challenges, whether the precedent lies in Ming Dynasty Suzhou or Miesian Chicago.



Peter Schaudt remarked: "A sense of being in a changing landscape—to me, that's what the Midwest is all about. From the prairie to the lake to wetlands, there's a constant change of seasonality... Landscape architects paint a picture month by month." Underlying the transitory tableaux of spring, summer, and fall is the firm armature of trunks, branches, and man-made structures that, as Midwesterners know, defines the view after autumn leaves fade. "I design for the winter first," says Hoerr. "That's when you understand the bones of a garden, which shape its forms and spaces over time." An image framed by a gateway, an outstretched limb, or a terrarium pane grants us the illusion of stopping nature in her tracks.

# CHAPTER 4 Time Travel

## Past to Present

## Season to Season

# Country Retreat

HIGHLAND PARK, ILLINOIS 1991 and 2010

"You knew that I was a restless man," Chicago stockbroker Abraham G. Becker told his friend and landscape architect, Jens Jensen. Which is why, the designer wrote, "Peace was my uppermost thought in planning [Becker's] estate." That project began in 1920, when Jensen advised his client to buy twenty acres on a bluff above Lake Michigan as the site for a country getaway. Sensitive composition, he promised, would create a pastorale of shady woodland, sunlit meadow, and tranquil water. The eminent Chicago architect Howard Van Doren Shaw chimed in with a compound whose English Vernacular understatement echoed the calm horizontality of Prairie Style ideals.

A succession of later residents sporadically "modernized" the house, to sometimes dubious effect, and yet most of the surroundings escaped destruction. Of course, as can happen with any aging garden, undergrowth stealthily blurred the contours of sculptured outcrops. Focal trees decayed. Stairs crumbled. Paths eroded. A couple of outlying acres fell prey to subdivision. In the early 1990s, the then-owner enlisted Doug Hoerr and naturalist Stephen Christy in "a rescue mission" to restore neglected woods and meadow as well as an orchard adjacent to a large formal garden—one of a surprising number of geometric beds for vegetables and flowers that Jensen produced at clients' behest.

Hoerr got his own chance to juggle naturalism and formality, history and modernity, after the property changed hands yet again, in 2007. The couple that purchased it commissioned H. Gary Frank Architects to extend the lake front of the main residence, which led to the addition of a pool, terraces, and various outbuildings in need of sympathetically revised landscapes. As Jensen had before him, Hoerr modulated plantings and structures to blend the orderly outlines of domesticity into nature's broader brushwork. The finished results of this fastidious artistry—deftly pruning gnarled hawthorns to reveal their intricate tracery, scouting out stone from the same Wisconsin quarry Jensen used—look deceptively simple, inevitable in retrospect. Near the pool house, for example, just before the wooded bluff plunges into a ravine, Hoerr melded a serpentine garden wall into a classic arched gateway. That one fluid gesture signals abiding peace.

**The restored front facade, ABOVE, looks much as it did in the 1920s when the back, LEFT, was photographed. Doug Hoerr's concave stair mediates between arches, the round entry court, and a path curving into the Prairie School landscape. Farther from the house, naturalism prevails in structures like these steps, OPPOSITE, which Hoerr grafted onto extant Jens Jensen rockwork. PREVIOUS PAGES: The master's beloved native limestone graces a new garden wall.**

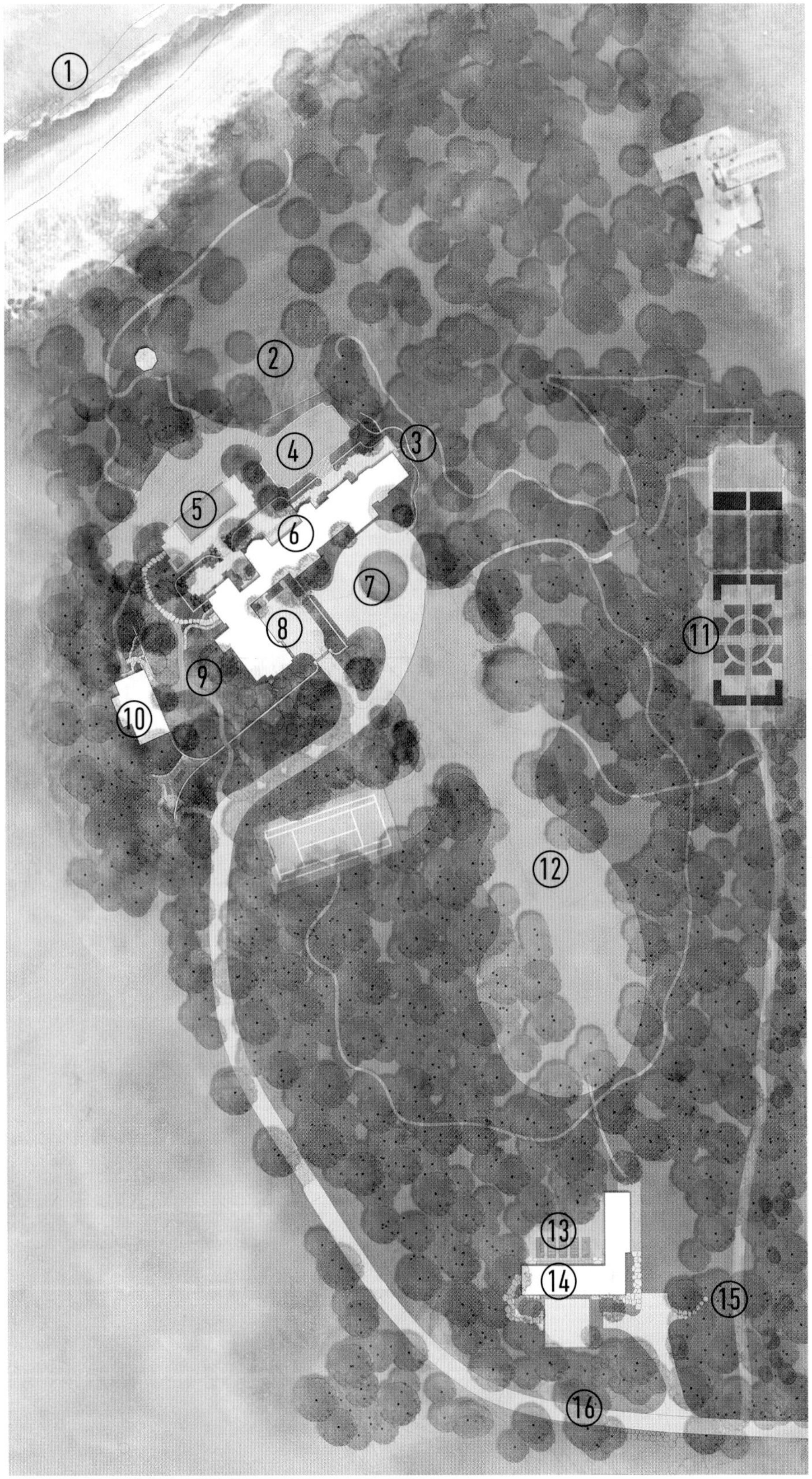

Stylishly relaxed planting accords with modern masonry in the informal Prairie idiom. ABOVE: 'Brookside' hardy geraniums sprawl beside the grass-jointed path, and 'Limelight' hydrangeas swerve uphill to embrace a brick wall. Smokebush (*Cotinus coggygria*) dominates the sloping lawn between terraces.

1 Lake Michigan
2 Bluff
3 Original Jensen walls
4 Formal lawn
5 Outdoor pool
6 Main house
7 Entry court
8 Garage court
9 Walled garden
10 Indoor pool with roof garden
11 Formal gardens
12 Sunset meadow
13 Vegetable garden/greenhouse
14 Carriage house
15 Service road
16 Main entry drive

Hoerr Schaudt collaborated on an extensive twenty-first-century enlargement of the house by architect H. Gary Frank, RIGHT, in the spirit of Howard Van Doren Shaw's original design. The circular staircase to the pool, ABOVE, recalls a recurrent feature in early twentieth-century landscapes by Edwin Lutyens, Shaw's influential English contemporary. Contrasting mounds of 'Green Velvet' boxwood and 'Powis Castle' artemisia recall Lutyens's frequent horticultural collaborator, Gertrude Jekyll.

Jensen's signature Prairie School picturesque has overshadowed the formal classicism he occasionally employed for both public and private clients. Examples include a 1908 circular rose garden in Chicago's Humboldt Park and a rectangular, walled plot on the Becker estate, OPPOSITE. Rescued from decay, the latter now comprises a cruciform parterre aglow with blue catmint (*Nepeta racemosa* 'Walker's Low') and silvery lamb's ear (*Stachys byzantina* 'Countess Helen von Stein'), both Jekyll standbys. A rustic arbor, ABOVE, supports wisteria and climbing roses.

The new garage addition, ABOVE, has courtyard walls and gates by Hoerr Schaudt in a neo-Shavian manner approved by the Highland Park Historic Preservation Commission. Brickwork matches that of the house, and the Arts and Crafts flavor of strap hinges, spindles, and other joinery recalls Shaw's own aesthetic leaning. Similar materials and details recur in walls and gates outside the vintage coach house, ABOVE AND BELOW RIGHT, now converted into guest quarters and a residence for the estate manager and gardener. OPPOSITE, CLOCKWISE FROM LEFT: Another variation on period gate vocabulary appears in an arched portal through the sinuous wall adjoining the new indoor swimming pool. Hoerr's masonry—in this case Wisconsin limestone laid seam-face-out in canonic Jensen style—bends and curves upward to screen the green-roofed pool house. Identical limestone visually binds glass pavilion to garden wall.

# University of Chicago

CHICAGO 2004–2012



In vintage photos, the Main Quadrangles at the University of Chicago present a late-nineteenth-century Anglophile vision of Matthew Arnold's "dreaming spires," lush greenswards, and stately paths for contemplative strolls. As the campus expanded, these central spaces remained its cultural, ceremonial heart. But by the time the university invited Hoerr Schaudt to undertake a landscape renovation, the quads below the spires looked far from dreamy. Rumbling thoroughfares for cars and trucks had replaced grand axial walkways and plantings laid out by the Olmsted brothers in the early 1900s. The structure of another Olmsted showpiece, Botany Pond, survived, although its profusion of specimen flora, which originally doubled as open-air laboratory and ornamental garden, had long since been swept away by curricular and budgetary reforms.

Hoerr Schaudt kicked off the revival of lost pomp and circumstance, pedestrian friendliness, and vegetation by narrowing the streets into broad pathways—still wide enough to accommodate the occasional off-hour delivery vehicle. Raising the former roadbed to the level of adjacent lawns eliminated curbs, a barrier to physical accessibility and visual flow. Instead of asphalt, new masonry pavement nods to time-honored English collegiate prototypes. "A dense limestone seemed the appropriate match for the neo-Gothic buildings here," Schaudt explained. "We based the striped patterning on old carriageways in Oxford and Cambridge, except our center stripe exploits current technology. It's a porous concrete that filters stormwater into sandy subsoil instead of city sewers." For most members of the academic community, however, this centerline marks their version of a red carpet—the route where kilted pipers lead annual processions of arriving freshmen and departing graduates.

On either side of the walkway, Hoerr Schaudt has provided for four-season horticultural spectacles: around and within Botany Pond to the east, and throughout Hull Court to the west. Because the idea of ecologically instructive gardens had taken on fresh urgency, Hoerr says, "We worked within the historic design shapes to enhance biodiversity." Hull now displays a rich mix of native prairie and savanna natives. Vibrant colors and textures satisfy another design goal: "Detail that resonates up close, on an individual level." No need to spell this out to the mallard ducks, red-eared slider turtles, or the dozen species of dragon- and damselflies in residence as tenure-track pond life.

**Chicago architect Henry Ives Cobb laid out the quadrangles in 1890 as a strictly pedestrian zone. During the 1930s, landscape architect Beatrix Farrand proposed barring vehicles from the roads that had usurped Cobb's axial paths. Hoerr Schaudt updated her unrealized idea, replacing the street with a grand walkway, OPPOSITE. Here, an academic procession is piped through Hull Gate ABOVE: New lawns and paths sweep across historic Snell-Hitchcock Quad.**

THE COLLEGE

Midway between Hull Gate and Harper Memorial Library, ABOVE, the north-south walk bisects a pedestrian roundabout shaded by red maples. When a preliminary site assessment revealed that the quads rest on a prehistoric lakebed, Peter Schaudt decided to treat stormwater by filtering it through the sandy substrate. The walkways' limestone paving blocks frame oblong panels of permeable concrete that absorbs runoff. Horticulturally diverse plantings such as those at Botany Pond, LEFT, reinforce the significance of the entire 217-acre campus as a botanic garden, officially designated as such in 1997 by the American Public Gardens Association.

Restoration of the quad outside the 1912 library, ABOVE, provided the opportunity to correct an awkward kink that had long marred the classic, otherwise axial approach from the north, BELOW. Hoerr Schaudt subtly jogged secondary walks to create the illusion of a symmetrical crossing. Imperceptibly raising center of the quad and deploying low hedges at key junctions also helped to mask the fact that Harper's immovable entrance remains slightly off-center.

# Garfield Park Conservatory

CHICAGO 2005



The pioneering conservatory that Jens Jensen designed for Garfield Park in 1905 still radiates originality. Scornful of pretentious Crystal Palace wannabes, Jensen modeled his structure on a Midwestern haystack. Rather than staging potted plants in formation like ballroom debutantes, the usual greenhouse etiquette back then, he arranged an indoor landscape as fluidly naturalistic as the meadows and lagoons he conjured up throughout the park. Within his conservatory, visitors marveled at exuberant drifts of flora growing "wild" on the banks of a prairie waterfall, as if some Illinois Eden had magically taken shelter under glass.

A visitor today might assume that this spell has never been lifted, thanks to the Chicago Park District's faithful restoration of the conservatory in the 1990s, after decades of decay had ravaged Garfield Park and adjacent neighborhoods. But when the park administrators chose Doug Hoerr to create a garden outside the greenhouse, client and designer agreed that a slavish Jensen reproduction made no sense. For starters, the twelve-acre site—Jensen's own makeover of pleasure grounds planned by William Le Baron Jenney in 1871—had largely been stripped of historic features. More important, though, Hoerr says, "The City wanted a learning garden that welcomed everyone, a park without edges that would help kick-start a 'green renaissance' in this whole part of town."

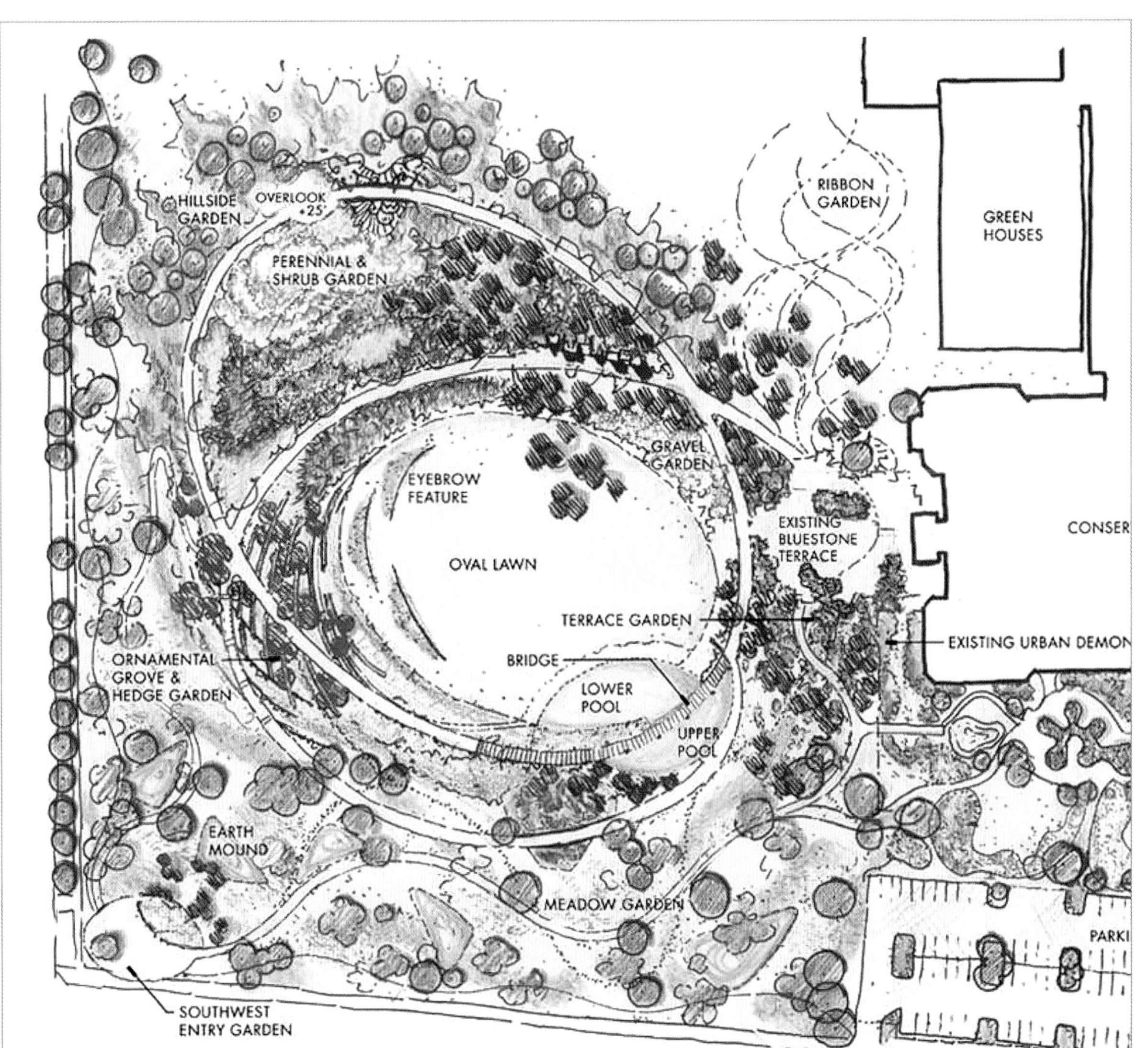

Hoerr's layout avoids outdoor rooms walled off by horticultural style, such as a French parterre or a Japanese Zen garden. Here, areas that address everyday urban-garden challenges—shadows cast by the building next door, sun-baked soil in a windowbox—flow into each other; annuals mingle with perennials and vegetables, and foliage spills onto gravel. These "soft segues," as Hoerr calls them, play off an elliptical lawn, his riff on Garfield Park's lost grassy oval, another Jensen leitmotif. Sinuous paths evoke Midwestern stream beds, and a lily-pond cascade reprises the Conservatory waterfall. Grassy new hillocks near the pond offer mysterious terrain to explore. They also look back to the region's indigenous tribes, who focused their communities on ceremonial mounds.

The modern metropolis unapologetically asserts itself in rebar vine trellises, sheet-pile retaining walls, and recycled-concrete pavers. Hoerr refrained from planting any trees that might screen nearby apartment houses or the L tracks along the park's southern boundary. "Why pretend that we're in some suburb on the North Shore?" Hoerr says. "Instead of shutting the world out, we're inviting the world in."

This photograph, BELOW, shows the conservatory in 1908, the year it opened. Jens Jensen designed it with Prairie School architects Schmidt, Garden & Martin.

Water lilies, pickerelweed, and aquatic cannas thrive in the Lower Pool, OPPOSITE, while red switch grass (*Panicum virgatum* 'Rotstrahlbusch') blankets the hill beyond the footbridge. A passing L train forms part of the backdrop, ABOVE LEFT, along with elephant ear, sumac, and papyrus. BELOW LEFT: Visitors are welcome to sit, recline, or climb on nearby rocks. PREVIOUS PAGES: The curved bridge, pools, and paths echo the oval of Jensen's original lawn.

As client, the Chicago Park District asked Doug Hoerr to avoid the stylistically or culturally defined "rooms" favored by many botanic gardens, and instead to plan a series of "experience zones" shaped by topography, paths, moisture, shade, and sun. Youngsters investigate a complex pond habitat, LEFT, from the dry land of a stone-paved bank. Perennial crimson-flowered mountain fleece (*Persicaria amplexicaulis* 'Firetail') happily adapts to waterside conditions. Japanese irises wade in the Upper Pool near a playground, ABOVE LEFT.

The well-drained hillside Gravel Garden, by contrast, RIGHT, is home to drought-tolerant vegetation. Japanese garden juniper (*Juniperus procumbens*), lavender, 'Autumn Joy' sedum, and 'Golden Sword' yucca sprawl below tall 'Emerald Green' arborvitae and an Amur maple flashing orange fall foliage. BELOW: Hawthorn limbs overhang rust red, industrial-strength retaining walls that divide a berm. BOTTOM: Ash trees stand out against sculptural turfed hummocks.

# Illinois Institute of Technology

CHICAGO 1998–2007



One of design history's unlikeliest hybrids sprouted in the 1940s and 1950s, when Bauhaus transplant Ludwig Mies van der Rohe, then IIT's director of architecture, joined forces with Alfred Caldwell, a late-blooming Prairie School landscape architect trained by Jens Jensen. The vibrant contrast of Caldwell's freeform scattering of native trees against the International Style precision of Mies's steel-and-glass geometry set a brave new standard for contemporary groves of academe.

Sadly, over the next half century, IIT also came to exemplify urban blight. The surrounding South Side neighborhood deteriorated. Rust marred ill-maintained campus landmarks. Extensive later construction outside the Miesian precinct felt marooned on the far side of traffic-clogged State Street, unsightly parking lots, and a looming elevated train line. Caldwell's ubiquitous American elms succumbed to disease, and equally prominent honey locusts expired at the end of their fifty-year lifespan. Alarmed by dwindling enrollment, college administrators pondered relocation outside the city.

"Folks who went to school there in the Fifties would say, 'This place was all forest!'" Peter Schaudt recalled. "But generations after them saw a wasteland." In 1998, Schaudt collaborated with landscape architect Michael Van Valkenburgh on an IIT master plan that invoked Mies and Caldwell's sylvan rus in urbe as a means of revitalizing the present-day community's pride of place. Entrusted with translating those concepts into on-campus reality, Schaudt decided that his mantra should be "Restraint—to make change that's bold, powerful, and yet never jarring." He successfully battled for permission to clear whole blocks of public parking from State Street, and planted meandering Caldwellian clumps of trees. He wanted it to look "as though birds dropped the seeds—to visually connect both flanks of the boulevard and blur the L."

His boldest move focused on an abandoned two-acre construction site in front of Mies's local masterpiece, S. R. Crown Hall, home to IIT's architecture department. Undergraduates had long ago adopted the vacant lot as an impromptu playing field. Schaudt sculpted the level ground into a gently sunken oblong with sloped sides to catch errant soccer balls and Frisbees. Open to the sky, Crown Hall Field now pays abstract homage to Jensen's signature forest clearings. New limestone benches mimic a dimensional module drawn from the Miesian canon. Schaudt observed, "It's subtle, but I love the idea that some student might do a double-take and say, 'Aha! There's something amazing going on here.'"

**While Peter Schaudt's graphic limestone slabs along State Street, OPPOSITE, honor the modernist geometry of landmarks like Mies van der Rohe's Siegel Hall, built in 1956, they also mark new edges for the reconfigured Crown Hall field. The main open space on campus, that sunken lawn rises gently to accommodate an existing grove of honey locust trees. LEFT: Foliage lining State Street, once again a vital campus spine, parallels elevated train tracks.**

OF TECHNOLOGY
PRITZK

Realignment of Federal Street, west of State, permitted the conversion of a mature linden allée, OPPOSITE, into a popular gathering place. The trees shade benches and crushed-gravel paving near architect Walter Netsch's Galvin Library, 1962. A photo from the 1970s, FAR LEFT, shows Mies's Crown Hall, 1956, in the foreground of two flat acres extending north to the master's Perlstein Hall, 1945. NEAR LEFT: Schaudt embedded seating into the new slopes of Crown Hall Field. BELOW: An homage to Alfred Caldwell's informal prairie spirit, open, multistemmed serviceberries (*Amelanchier* x *grandiflora*) display fall color.

ARMOUR MISSION

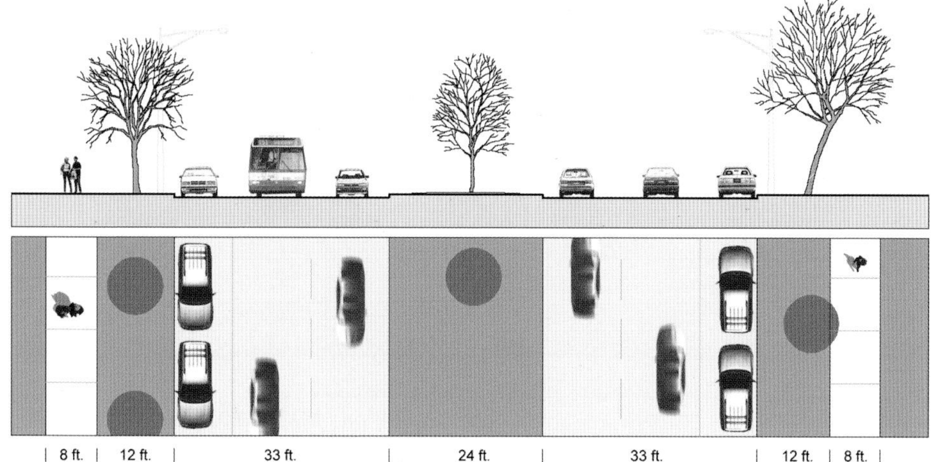


"BEFORE" - STATE STREET SECTION AND PLAN

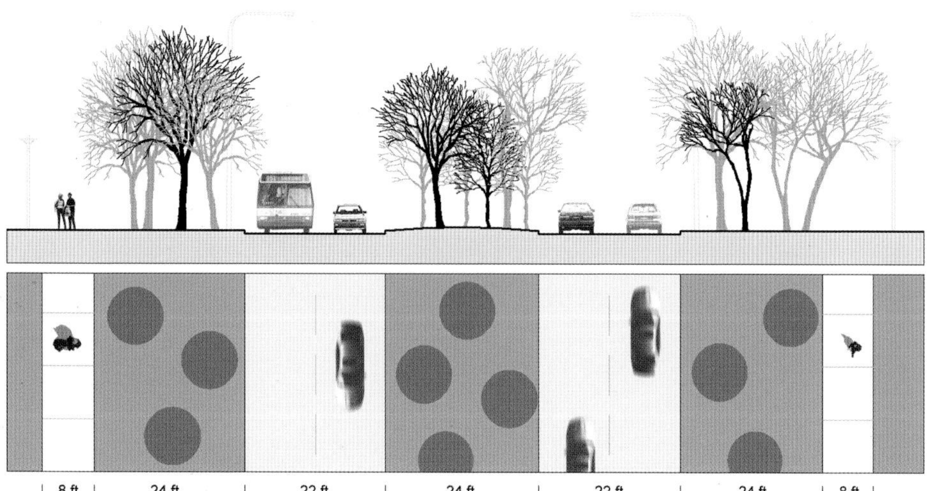


"AFTER" - STATE STREET SECTION AND PLAN

Under a perforated-steel canopy in Helmut Jahn's State Street Village, a residence hall completed in 2003, OPPOSITE, airy white birches contrast with broad squares of purple-leaf wintercreeper (*Euonymous fortunei* 'Coloratus'). The recessed courtyard faces State Street and Crown Hall Field. ABOVE: Formal bosques in all three of the building's open courts alternate with looser Caldwellian plantings along the sidewalk (L trains run behind the linear complex). The birches also nod to taller shade trees in the streetscape. Before-and-after diagrams, LEFT, illustrate the narrowed roadway and fuller plantings that have recast auto-dominated State Street, TOP LEFT, as a gracious, pedestrian-friendly boulevard, TOP RIGHT.

# Chervon International Trading Company

Nanjing, People's Republic of China 2005–2007



Looking down at this corporate headquarters from the air, a Western visitor could easily think that some master calligrapher had drawn its outlines in a few sure strokes. A campus tour only reinforces this impression, because the patterning of symbolism and utility within the 7.5-acre urban site is as dynamically articulate as the characters brushed onto an Asian scroll. The bold modernity of Hoerr Schaudt's design, a close collaboration with architects Perkins+Will, underscores Chervon's innovative approach to manufacturing electric power tools for the world market. At the same time, traditional textures and meanings layered throughout the facility attest to the company credo: "Born in China, Growing Globally."

Peter Schaudt dove into this venture by researching the history of Chinese scholars' gardens, exquisite courtyard microcosms of wild terrain whose idealized "mountain peaks," "lakes," and "forests" were intended for connoisseurs to savor like paintings. "After hitting the books at home," Schaudt said, "we visited the real thing in Suzhou, another major city in East China." Preserved landmarks such as the Master of Nets Garden, a Southern Song Dynasty gem, prompted abstract reinterpretations of venerable themes at Chervon.

Cobblestone mosaics resurfaced in the paved lobby. Ancient zigzag garden bridges, an inducement to meditative lingering, inspired the staggered multilevel outdoor boardwalks that connect all five corporate departments at Nanjing. An alternative interior circulation spine runs straight through the whole complex, a symbol for "the direct path of globalization," according to Ralph Johnson, who headed the Perkins+Will project design team.

Together, he and Schaudt achieved the breakthrough of erecting Nanjing's first green roofs. The uppermost of these two turfed tiers, vast enough to shelter most of the site, slopes to suggest a mountainside. Latticelike cutouts admit sun and rain to the lower roof, where employees can relax on benches or run laps around a track. Like the office windows below, this roof's open parapets overlook the tranquil geometry of circular islands dotting angular ponds and a stylized plum-tree orchard that, figuratively at least, buffers traffic noise and smog.

A modern corporate headquarters, OPPOSITE, encases islands, cobblestones, and other canonic elements of Chinese garden design. The young dawn redwoods (*Metasequoia glyptostroboides*) on islets in the entrance courtyard pool descend from an ancestor in Hubei province revered as "Shui-sa," or water fir. BELOW: The 743,000-square-foot green roof tilts for visibility from the ground.

Peter Schaudt and principal Rob Gray visited historic scholars' retreats in Suzhou on a search for themes to inform their collaboration with architect Ralph Johnson. Walkways across water in the Chervon complex, ABOVE, recall antique bridges at sites such as the Ming Dynasty Humble Administrator's Garden, NEAR RIGHT; and stylized lakes like the Master of Nets Garden's Rosy Cloud Pool, FAR RIGHT.

Abstraction streamlines the antique "mountain-water" scenery exemplified by the Lion Grove Garden, FAR LEFT, into spare twenty-first-century topography. The lobby pavilion's metal shaft, a symbol of tool technology, NEAR LEFT, pierces a sedum slope. ABOVE: A linear woodland and orchard shield the corporate campus from the street.

Traditional herringbone-patterned wood paves the Chervon "bridge," RIGHT, which traverses multiple levels on its course from one end of the facility to the other. Besides evoking the serenity of ancient water features, large pools supply evaporative cooling during Nanjing's notorious "furnace city" summers.

Within the cloister-like employee courtyard overlooked by offices, ABOVE, informally contoured groundcover "islands" surround groves of cherry trees and pines. Artfully positioned boulders double as sculpture and seating. One story below the covered walkway, a waterfall references another mainstay of classic Chinese gardens. Wavy paving continues the theme. RIGHT: Emphatically angular architecture provides "mountain peaks" for the emblematic landscapes. OPPOSITE, FROM TOP: A large area of the green roof overhead is perforated to let sunlight and rainfall reach this lower green roof in the staff recreation area, which includes a running track. Diagrams illustrate the linkage of five work zones through walkways and shared access to water features and gardens.

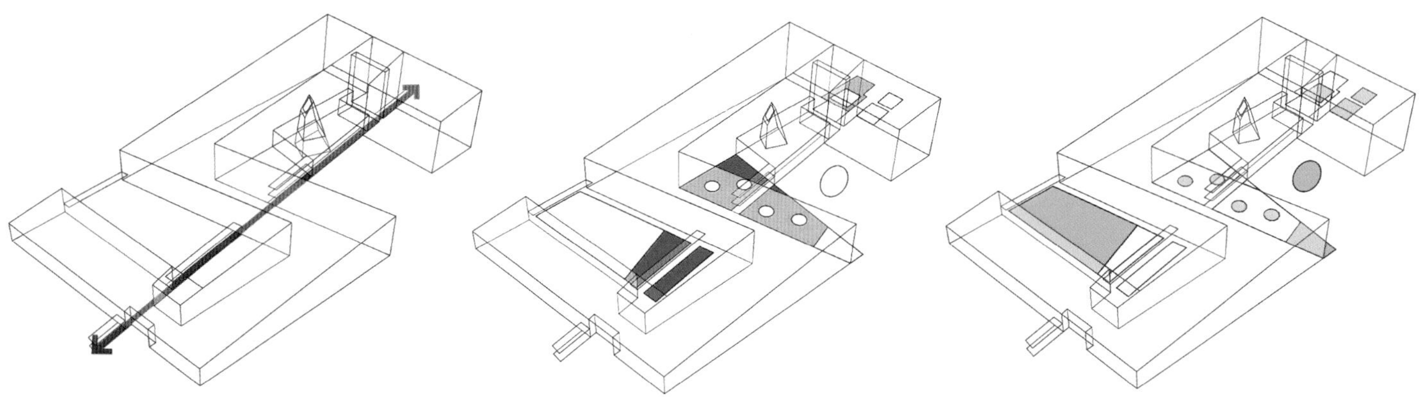

Primary circulation spine

Water elements

Landscape zones

# Cascade House Driveway Plantings

CHICAGO'S NORTH SHORE 2007

No two trips along the winding approach to Cascade House are ever quite the same. Although the desired overall effect for these driveway plantings was "Midwest natural," as Doug Hoerr terms it, his clients asked for a more intriguing range of plant varieties than the usual North Shore shortlist allows. And they specifically requested "seasonal surprises." An intensive search ensued for regionally appropriate plants "with the right amount of quirkiness," Hoerr explains.

The easygoing charm of the result—in all four seasons—belies Hoerr Schaudt's horticultural acumen. While pacing trees and shrubs to delay the full reveal of the house and its bluff-side views of Lake Michigan, the designers strategically deployed perennials, grasses, and bulbs for tantalizing diversions en route. Anyone who heads in from the street through the West Border and moves on to the North Border enjoys an exciting journey, whether or not he can rattle off botanical names.

The roll call includes the March-blooming Lenten rose *Helleborus* x *hybridus* Metallic Blue Lady,' whose deep purple petals have an arresting steely sheen; the meadow rue *Thalictrum aquilegifolium* 'Black Stockings,' a froth of lavender June flowers atop ebony stems; the bugbane *Cimicifuga simplex* 'Brunette,' so called for the dusky purple leaves beneath its white bottlebrushes of September bloom; purple love grass, *Eragrostis spectabilis*, which turns from light green to brilliant pink in the fall; and the coneflower *Echinacea purpurea* 'Virgin,' with white summer daisies that leave behind dark brown seed heads to punctuate wintry scenes.

Similar connoisseurship and precision went into the bulb timetable. "We planted at least 30,000 bulbs here," says principal Simon Prunty, "and they play vital roles in bridging seasons." February's giant snowdrops, *Galanthus elwesii*, get a jump on spring near the front door. April's Siberian squills, *Scilla siberica*, sprinkle blue stars across the front lawn, while intriguingly green-centered white *Narcissus* 'Misty Glen' brightens the North Border. The daffodils are followed by May's azure tide of the quamash *Camassia leichtlinii* 'Blue Danube,' which helps to fill the gap before perennials' midsummer glory. As that extravaganza winds down, eye-catching alliums persevere well into August.

Up in higher layers of the composed woodland, flowers on Eastern redbud trees, multistemmed shadblow serviceberry, Merrill magnolias, Sargent cherry trees, and Japanese tree lilacs embellish the winter-to-spring transition. 'Limelight' hydrangeas and hardy roses like 'Fru Dagmar Hastrup' and 'Knockout' provide summer-long color. Inevitably, in this climate, deciduous foliage rules over autumn. But amid the proverbial blaze of sugar maple and swamp white oak, less expected attractions glimmer: the lemon-yellow flicker of quaking aspen leaves, the purple gleam of hackberry fruits.

In summer, lilac-colored 'Superba' Chinese astilbe and yellow 'The Rocket' ligularia, OPPOSITE, glow near the front door. ABOVE: Early spring sees scarlet-flowering quince (*Chaenomeles speciosa*) blaze beside a path.

As at the Tiffany Celebration Garden, evergreens maintain a solid enclosure. But along the drive at Cascade House, it is free-spirited specimens rather than regimented groups that command attention. Feathery 'Grey Owl' juniper, shaggy yew, and weeping white pine stand out as sculpture, pure and simple.

Each season stages tableaux beside the driveway. Grape hyacinth and camassia, TOP LEFT, mix a vibrant spring palette of blues. Farther along the drive, approaching the circle in front of the house in summer, TOP RIGHT, a tall swamp white oak, at left, stands over a compact mugo pine and a clump of 'Dark Towers' penstemon in flower. By fall, BOTTOM LEFT, the penstemon foliage has turned claret red, and 'October Skies' aster floats lavender-blue daisies against spreading 'Grey Owl' juniper. Beyond the bronzy spires of astilbe seed heads and quaking aspens' white bark, a sugar maple turns orange. Come winter, BOTTOM RIGHT, the deep green mugo pine anchors a dried arrangement of ebony coneflower (*Echinacea*) seed heads and luminous, fine-textured blades of prairie dropseed (*Sporobolus heterolepis*). Wine-dark penstemon refuses to quit the show.

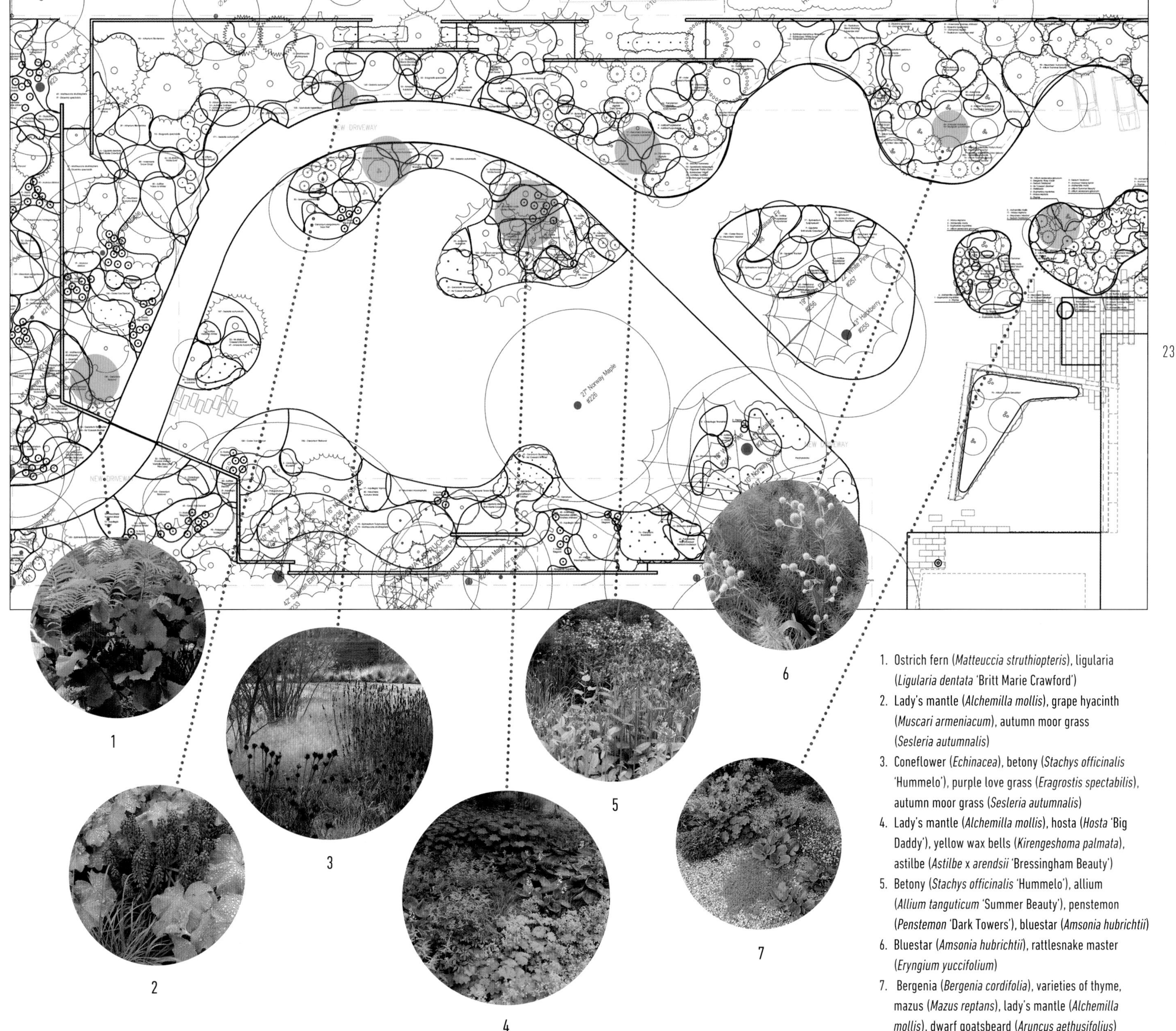


1. Ostrich fern (*Matteuccia struthiopteris*), ligularia (*Ligularia dentata* 'Britt Marie Crawford')
2. Lady's mantle (*Alchemilla mollis*), grape hyacinth (*Muscari armeniacum*), autumn moor grass (*Sesleria autumnalis*)
3. Coneflower (*Echinacea*), betony (*Stachys officinalis* 'Hummelo'), purple love grass (*Eragrostis spectabilis*), autumn moor grass (*Sesleria autumnalis*)
4. Lady's mantle (*Alchemilla mollis*), hosta (*Hosta* 'Big Daddy'), yellow wax bells (*Kirengeshoma palmata*), astilbe (*Astilbe* x *arendsii* 'Bressingham Beauty')
5. Betony (*Stachys officinalis* 'Hummelo'), allium (*Allium tanguticum* 'Summer Beauty'), penstemon (*Penstemon* 'Dark Towers'), bluestar (*Amsonia hubrichtii*)
6. Bluestar (*Amsonia hubrichtii*), rattlesnake master (*Eryngium yuccifolium*)
7. Bergenia (*Bergenia cordifolia*), varieties of thyme, mazus (*Mazus reptans*), lady's mantle (*Alchemilla mollis*), dwarf goatsbeard (*Aruncus aethusifolius*)

# The Podium, Nathan Phillips Square

TORONTO 2010

 Toronto's tomorrow looked rosy in ultramodern Nathan Phillips Square. Or so it seemed to Finnish architect Viljo Revell when he drew up his futuristic master plan for the twelve-acre square and the new city hall it framed. Distinguished out-of-towners who stopped by to see the mayor on official business would ascend an imposing curved ramp—wide enough for Queen Elizabeth II's limousine—and receive a ceremonial greeting on the square's elevated Podium, a plaza right outside City Hall. And if the Podium weren't hosting some dignitary, ordinary Torontonians and tourists would be welcome to stroll, relax, and sightsee amid its elegant landscape. This was the Podium that Revell envisioned when he died in 1964.

Completed by others a year later, much of the multilevel civic center lived up to Revell's hopes for hospitable, active, sculptural urban spaces. The three-acre Podium, alas, did not. Budget cuts ruled out any greenery, so the city settled for a desert of concrete-block paving. As gray and desolate in June as in December, this elevated platform—actually the roof over ground-floor facilities—had in effect been abandoned long before the City finally closed it off in the 1980s. The Podium remained inaccessible for more than a decade.

In 2007 Hoerr Schaudt, collaborating with PLANT Architect, Shore Tilbe Irwin + Partners, and Adrian Blackwell Urban Projects, won an international competition to revitalize aging Nathan Phillips Square. Phase one transformed the bleak Podium into a park so versatile, resilient, and hospitable that its aesthetic appeal now has no "off" season. With 40,000 square feet of vegetation, this is Canada's largest publicly accessible green roof garden, and it attracts a healthy share of Nathan Phillips Square's 1.5 million annual visitors. Rows

The square's upper-tier green roof, OPPOSITE, embraces both towers of City Hall with a public garden that is accessible all year round. In contrast to the concrete wasteland they replaced, emerging spring grasses and perennials, ABOVE, ground the flying saucer–like Council Chamber with lively color and texture.

Hilton

of oblong planting trays lay out a striped tapestry whose right angles set off City Hall's two curved towers and circular Council Chamber. Specifying tray modules in both four-inch and six-inch depths, for different soil profiles, enabled Hoerr Schaudt to weave together perennials, bulbs, and grasses that can cope with Toronto's climatic rigors as well as a broad spectrum of sun exposure.

This botanical mix was composed for abundant variations in seasonal color as well as year-round contrasts of height and texture scaled to the wide-open urban plateau. At ground level, even in winter, an extraordinary tonal range of sedums—more than 15 kinds—maps a calibrated sequence from yellow, orange, and chartreuse in the sunniest southwestern areas to red and purple in the northeast, where Revell's towers cast giant shadows across the podium. Such painterly effects, which shift from hour to hour, make it easy to see why the design team found inspiration in Paul Klee's abstract *Polyphony* (1932). The team's attention to chromatics foretells a bright future for the Podium. Of course, as Peter Schaudt noted, it's hard to predict when a spreading plant might color outside the lines.

Installation of deeper-than-normal soil trays meant that sedums, the tough but low-growing rooftop standby, could be joined by grasses and perennials, which provide greater heights that help to scale such a vast space, as well as winter interest. In summer, ABOVE RIGHT, feather reed grass (*Calamagrostis* x *acutiflora* 'Overdam'), lesser calamint (*Calamintha nepeta*), and hoary vervain (*Verbena stricta*) play equal roles around Adrian Blackwell benches. On a blustery winter day, however, RIGHT, the reed grass's four-foot plumes steal the limelight.

Before the green roof took root, ABOVE, the Podium presented a bleak tabula rasa. Its metamorphosis sprang from a 2007 competition-winning plan to revitalize all of Nathan Phillips Square. The multifirm entry included this drawing, RIGHT, which locates the Podium within the larger scheme.

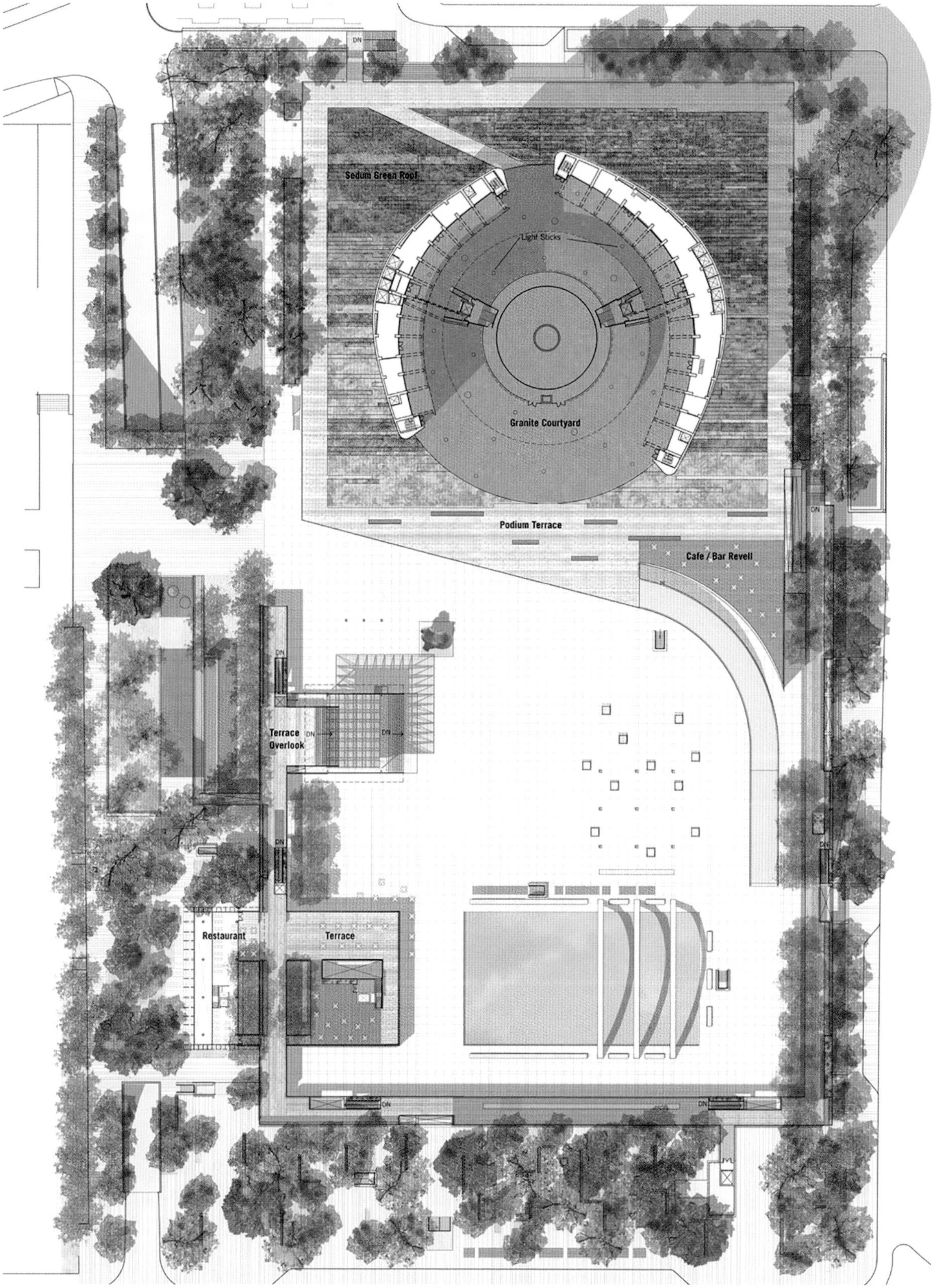

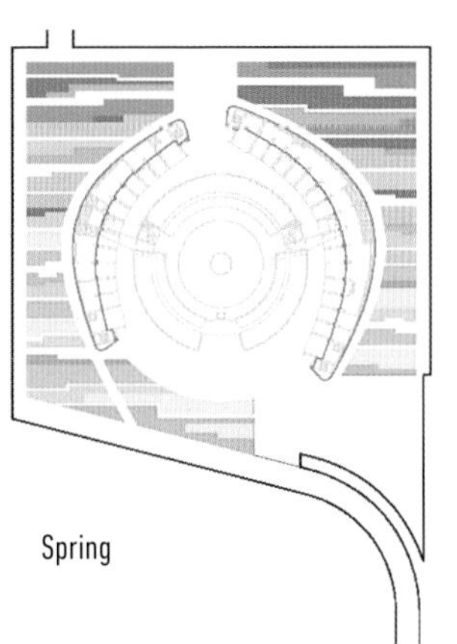


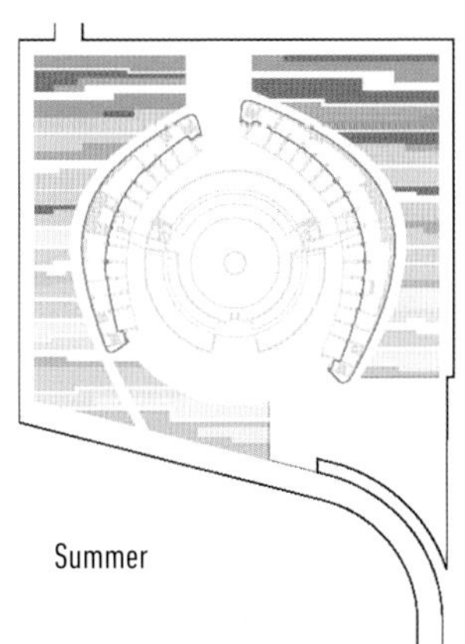


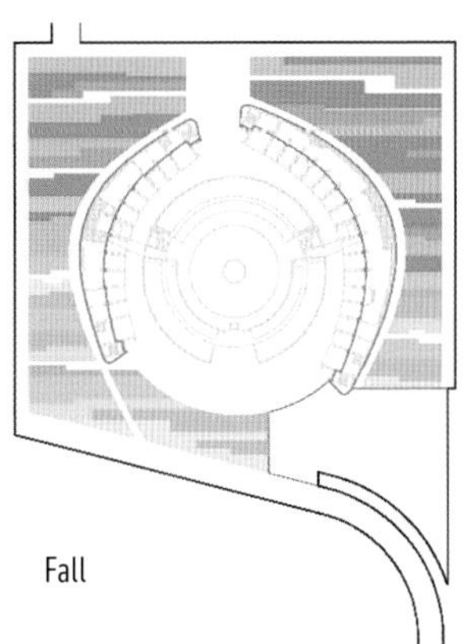


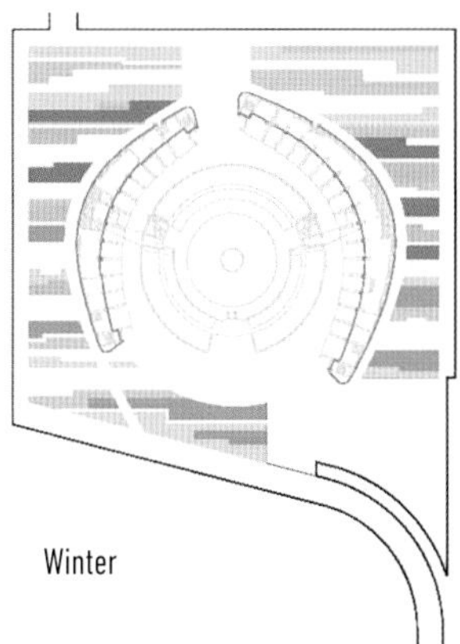


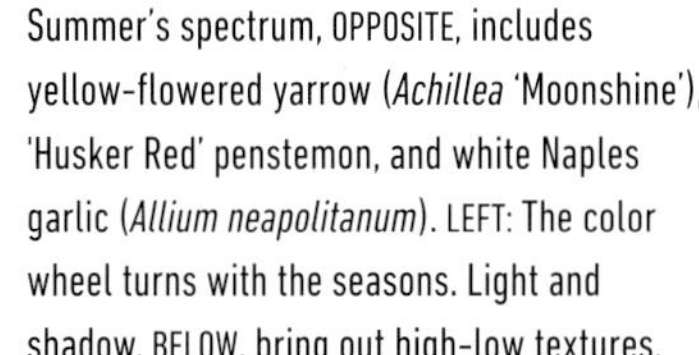

Summer's spectrum, OPPOSITE, includes yellow-flowered yarrow (*Achillea* 'Moonshine'), 'Husker Red' penstemon, and white Naples garlic (*Allium neapolitanum*). LEFT: The color wheel turns with the seasons. Light and shadow, BELOW, bring out high-low textures.

Bank of America
Stadium

# Bank of America Stadium

CHARLOTTE, NORTH CAROLINA 1996



Team colors—black, electric blue, and silver—have emblazoned the home of the Carolina Panthers ever since the 75,000-seat football stadium, designed by HOK, opened in 1996. But the NFL club's uptown Charlotte site also flaunts the unofficial color of Panthers Pride: green. "You might not think the team's owner, Jerry Richardson, would care about anything green besides the turf on the field," Peter Schaudt said. "And yet when he hired us to do eleven acres outside the building, Jerry told me, 'This has got to be a stadium in a park, not just another ballpark surrounded by asphalt.'" Richardson also demanded plantings that would look spectacular all football season long; i.e., from August preseason games through January's postseason finale.

Schaudt determined that only walkways flanked by stately trees could hold their own against the mass of Carolinas—now Bank of America—Stadium. Although deciduous trees could supply fall color in Charlotte's climate, he wanted something evergreen for the prime winter months: "But not just any evergreen. It had to be recognizably Southern." The ideal candidate, he decided, was native live oak *Quercus virginiana*, a stalwart in coastal regions of the Old South. Besides retaining shiny green leaves year round, except for a well-timed spring break, live oaks can top fifty feet in height, spread as far as one hundred feet, withstand hurricanes, and flourish for centuries.

Schaudt ran up against a big obstacle, however: "People in Charlotte said, 'Live oaks won't work this far inland. Wrong hardiness zone. Wrong soil.'" Undaunted, he phoned the legendary North Carolina horticulturist J. C. Raulston. "You'll be fine," Raulston advised. "Just find live oaks grown from acorns collected in northern Louisiana, which is almost the same zone as Charlotte. It doesn't matter then if those acorns germinate in California or Florida." After hauling in well-drained river soil to layer over the site's dense clay, Schaudt planted ninety-six live oaks from the "right" stock, raised at a Florida nursery. About seventeen feet tall and wide back then, those trees now measure roughly eight feet larger, and the parallel rows that ring the stadium have begun to join branches into imposing allées.

In 2014, during a $65 million stadium renovation, Jerry Richardson made it quite clear that if huge new escalator bays threatened a single live oak, the escalators—not the trees—would need to move.

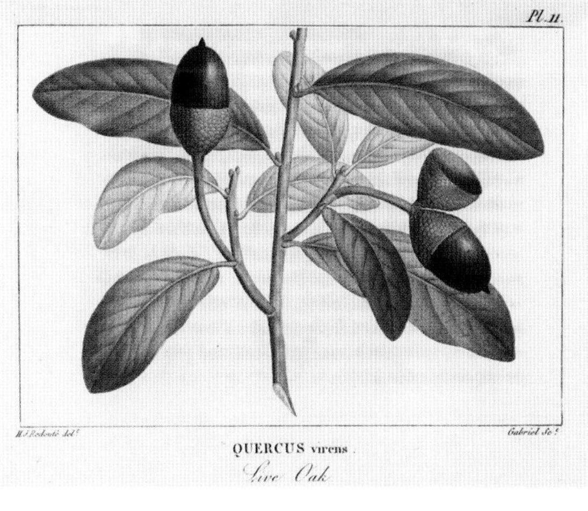


Allées of almost-evergreen southern live oak (*Quercus virginiana*) hug the stadium, OPPOSITE, ensuring a verdant canopy whenever football is in play. TOP RIGHT: Besides improving parking lot views, the tree-lined walks direct circulation to arena entrances and to adjacent grounds for picnics and walks. That landscape has been planted with dogwood, loblolly pine, crape myrtle and other natives. RIGHT: A detail from an 1812 print by botanical artist Pierre-Joseph Redouté depicts live-oak acorns.

RUSH UNIVERSITY
MEDICAL CENTER
EDWARD A. BRENNAN
ENTRY PAVILION

# Rush University Medical Center Terrarium

CHICAGO 2011



Acute hunger for a glimpse of nature—a freshly popped flower bud, a sunlit petal, a bright autumn leaf, a frosty twig—is a common side effect of hospitals' clinical sterility. Little wonder that research demonstrates the therapeutic effect of hospital gardens on patients, visitors, and staff. As an aid to healing, and as an emblem for the LEED sustainability of their monumental addition to Rush University's healthcare complex, architects Perkins+Will centered this new entry pavilion on a forty-foot-tall built-in terrarium.

The size and sculptural drama of this elliptical glass cone, which penetrates a green roof overhead, set it apart from classic terrariums. A more critical distinction, for Hoerr Schaudt's role in creating a landscape inside the transparent vessel, is the unglazed circular opening at its top. The typical terrarium has a solid cover to give plants a stable, controlled microclimate. But this "reverse terrarium," in architect Ralph Johnson's words, has no lid. Its inhabitants must contend with snow, wind, drought, and whatever else Chicago weather delivers—unlike the lobby surrounding the laminated-glass shell, which is tightly sealed to exclude human pathogens and irritants that might be carried in on gusts of outside air. "Doug and I approached the terrarium as a sort of cloister for plants," Peter Schaudt said. "Anybody passing by always has something interesting to look at."

Computer analysis of sunlight angles within the huge container revealed that its 477-square-foot floor would receive a mere 100–150 foot-candles, illumination too dim for most flora. Hoerr Schaudt planted shade-tolerant mosses, ferns, bulbs, and perennials in a hydrotech, lightweight soil mixture. For even moisture, spray nozzles and bubblers distribute water reclaimed from roof runoff. The desire for four-season appeal prompted the selection of deciduous trees, which had to be inserted through the terrarium's one three-by-six-foot door—upper stories around the roof garden precluded the use of a crane to hoist trees in from above. In Doug Hoerr's finished installation, the limbs of Allegheny serviceberry (*Amelanchier laevis*) and American ironwood (*Carpinus caroliniana*) overhang a dappled ground cover that includes broom moss (*Dicranum scoparium*), hart's-tongue fern (*Asplenium scolopendrium*), squill (*Scilla*), white trillium (*Trillium grandiflorum*), and Canada wild ginger (*Asarum canadense*). This capsule woodland promises no instant cures, but its beauty is a palliative that any nurse or doctor will endorse.

**An open top lets the three-story lobby terrarium, OPPOSITE, admit sun and weather to its in-vitro forest. ABOVE: The uncapped oculus and twin skylights project as garden sculpture on a sedum-clad roof terrace.**

 Terrarium residents include, CLOCKWISE FROM TOP LEFT, Allegheny serviceberry (*Amelanchier laevis*) in full bloom; eastern hop hornbeam (*Ostrya virginiana*) sporting female catkins; a carpet of various mosses; and squill (*Scilla*), a bulbous member of the asparagus family.

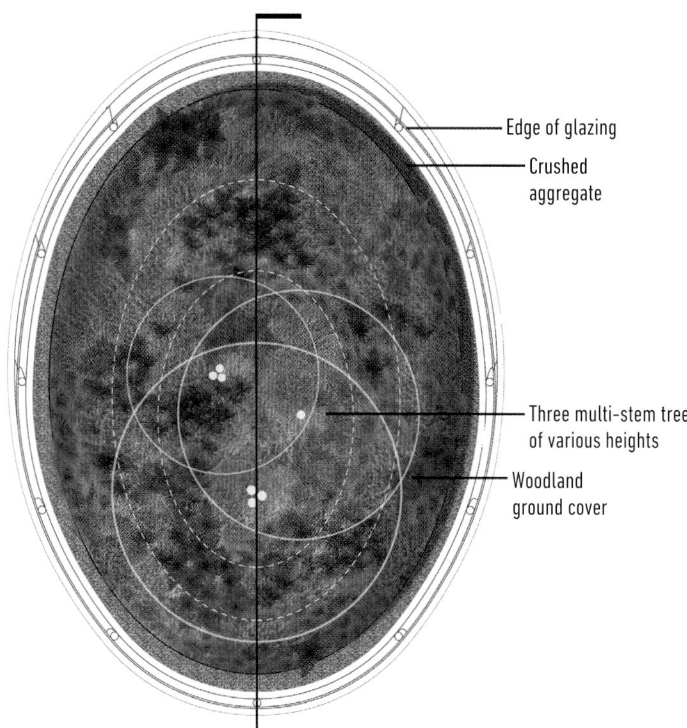


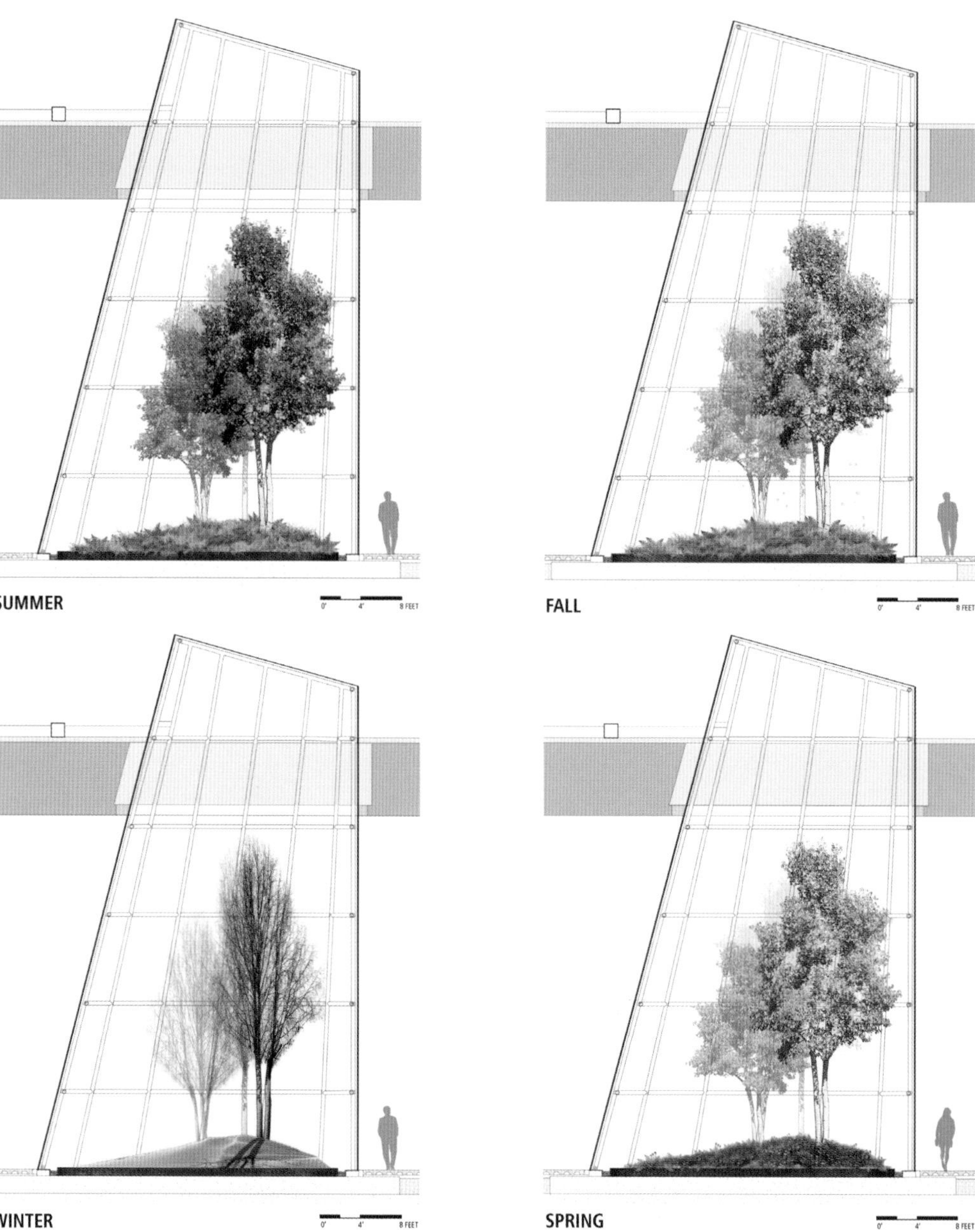


Spatial constraints and intensive light-level analysis narrowed Hoerr Schaudt's preliminary planting scheme, ABOVE, to small, upright trees and understory varieties adapted to relatively dim woodland-floor environments. RIGHT: Exposed to local climate conditions, trees undergo natural seasonal changes.

A laminated, low-iron-glass curtain wall, LEFT, seals off the surrounding lobby from possible external contamination. Donors' names are inscribed on eye-level panes. The grove of trees inside consists of two serviceberries and one eastern hop hornbeam. BELOW: In spring, white foamflower (*Tiarella cordifolia*) rises above the moss.

# A Photographer's Garden

WINNETKA, ILLINOIS 2012

The grainy sepia of gravel and stone, LEFT, underscores spring's luminous colors and lush textures. Allium, sedum, juniper, and catmint blur the edge of the front drive while amsonia, white pine, bottlebrush buckeye, ginkgo, and quaking aspen all but dance along a sinuous wall. By contrast, winter's monochrome stillness, ABOVE, brings line and structure into sharp focus.

Just as flowerbeds hit their Kodachrome peak, student gardeners are often instructed to shoot black-and-whites that focus on essential composition rather than "transient" color. Winter snowfalls demonstrate the same principle, at master-class level, in the carefully balanced landscape of light and shadow that Hoerr Schaudt designed for a photographer and her family. The house she and her husband commissioned from architects Booth Hansen is itself an exercise in modernist chiaroscuro. Dark zinc trim offsets pale stucco, accentuating the rectangular windows that Laurence Booth and Doug Hoerr conceived as all-season viewfinders. Whatever tones may wax and wane in nature, these apertures frame poetic contrasts between rational geometry and romantic terrain.

There's also a prosaic backstory: the property sits on low ground, and the local construction code required excavation for optimal stormwater storage. Hoerr Schaudt transfigured necessity into a design gesture. A serpentine sunken lawn rimmed by stone walls now meanders through the two-acre lot's deep frontage. Clustered shrubbery and trees advance and recede among drifts of naturalized bulbs and perennials, animating vistas, screening neighbors, and concealing much of the house from passersby.

The irregular pattern of adjacent public roads let Hoerr Schaudt install two driveways. From spring

through fall, the long front drive—an unobtrusive ribbon of gravel and grass—threads its way amid luxuriant plantings. But in winter, to avoid snowplow damage, access switches to the short rear drive. Both routes lead to a U-shaped entry courtyard centered on a two-story glass wall whose gridded panes reveal a helical staircase that parallels the curves outdoors. On the opposite side of the court, the oblique horizontal thrust of rough-cut megaliths interrupts precise ashlar pavers, asymmetrically balancing the picture while leaving it open to momentary shifts in hue and texture.

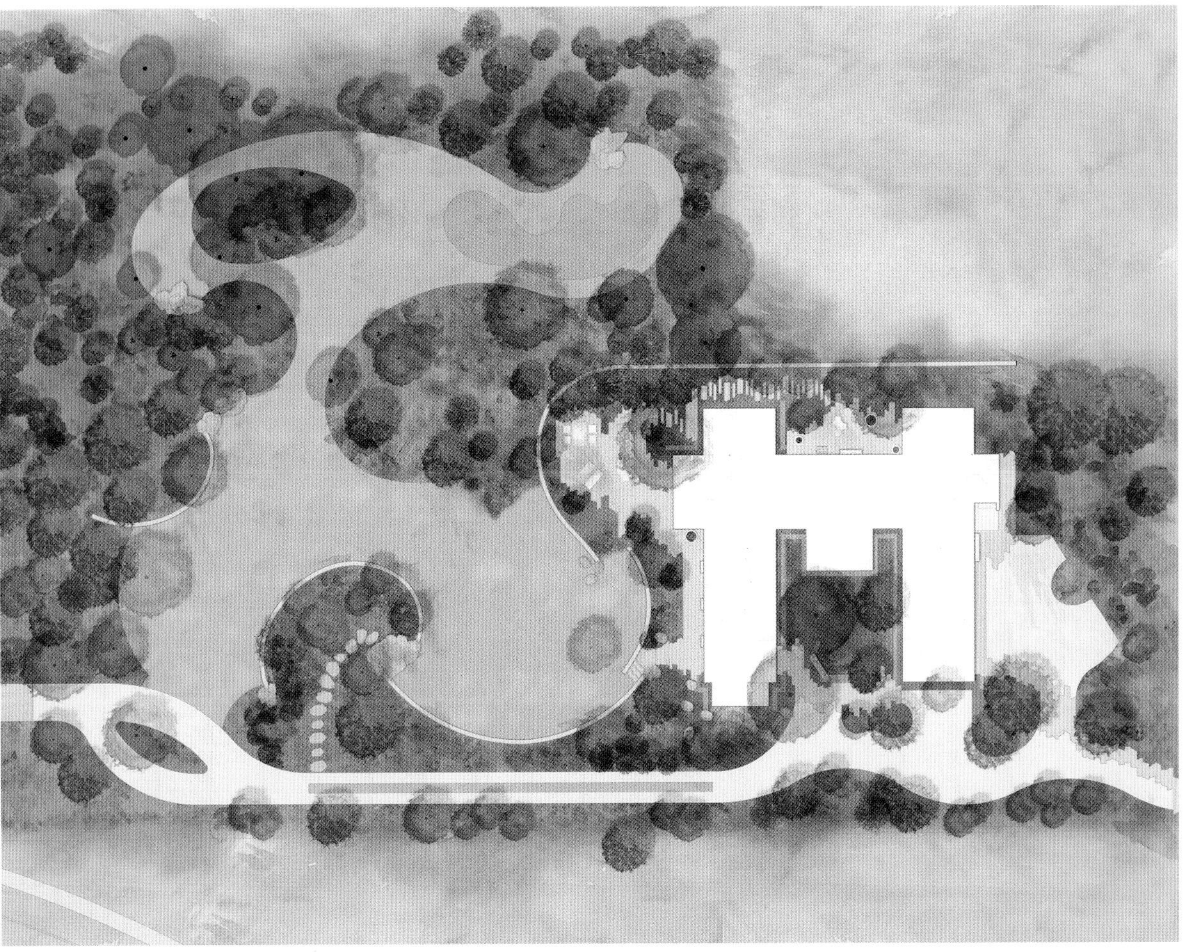

Cyclopean stone slabs gesture toward the front door, OPPOSITE, implying a full courtyard without blocking views from the interior stairway. Boxwood, pachysandra, hardy geranium, and rhododendron round out the sharp corners. A honey locust and a white pine softly veil the stucco-and-zinc facades. ABOVE LEFT: Hoerr Schaudt's arrangement of shrubs and trees bears in mind what the Japanese call "snow blossoms." TOP RIGHT: Walls at the back entrance play up the diverse foliage of yew, swamp white oak, and ostrich fern. In the site plan, ABOVE, the front driveway runs to the left of the house, the rear drive to the right.

The curved walls that emphatically contain the shallow swale of lawn, OPPOSITE, also suggest a tidal flow, sweeping the eye across the garden and making the property feel larger than it is. In the foreground, garnet barberry and mauve geranium intensify the electric purple of *Iris* 'Caesar's Brother.' THIS PAGE, FROM TOP: When approached via the front drive, the house is barely discernible through dense foliage. The rear entry wall displays the irregular herringbone stonework used throughout the landscape. A path between front drive and lawn rambles past spreading juniper, Russian sage, and lady's mantle.

# Tiffany Celebration Garden

GRANT PARK, CHICAGO 2009



Like one of those sundials inscribed, "I mark only the happy hours," this landscape celebrates momentous occasions as well as fleeting pleasures. A $1.25 million grant from the Tiffany & Co. Foundation ensured that the 28,000-square-foot civic garden—a short walk from Lake Michigan and Buckingham Fountain, the opulent centerpiece of 319-acre Grant Park—would carry out its mission in impeccable style. Doug Hoerr's design is at once ceremonious and intimate, romantic and pragmatic, making the site equally suitable for wedding processions and workday tête-à-têtes, benefit luncheons and twilight rambles. Rental proceeds from approved private functions serve the public good by funding maintenance here and in municipal projects elsewhere.

As the successor to Grant Park's early-twentieth-century South Rose Garden, this space gracefully emulates the symmetry of its Beaux-Arts setting. "This is a grand, axial space, as it always has been," says Hoerr Schaudt associate principal Steve Gierke. "If you approach from the south, the central paved promenade, the hedges, and the vine-swagged posts lead your eye to the fountain. Look the opposite way, and there's a beautiful vista of Museum Campus." The axis loosens up with serpentines of boxwood as fluid as the baroque waterworks to the north and the vast lake to the east.

The undulating borders, capped by a green arc at either end, delineate a series of secluded niches and open-air rooms. When these spaces aren't furnishing handsome backdrops for temporary party tents, catering stations, and photo ops, they encourage casual parkgoers to slow down for a panoramic skyline view or a close-up of the garden's nearly 7,600 annuals and perennials, 95 vines, and 270 flowering trees and shrubs. Summer brides, of course, have their pick of roses, lilies, hydrangeas, and phlox to pose against, but Hoerr Schaudt has compiled a plant list that guarantees nonstop horticultural delight for any garden visitor from spring through winter.

Tiffany's early show features crab apples, iris, and peonies, introducing a three-season color

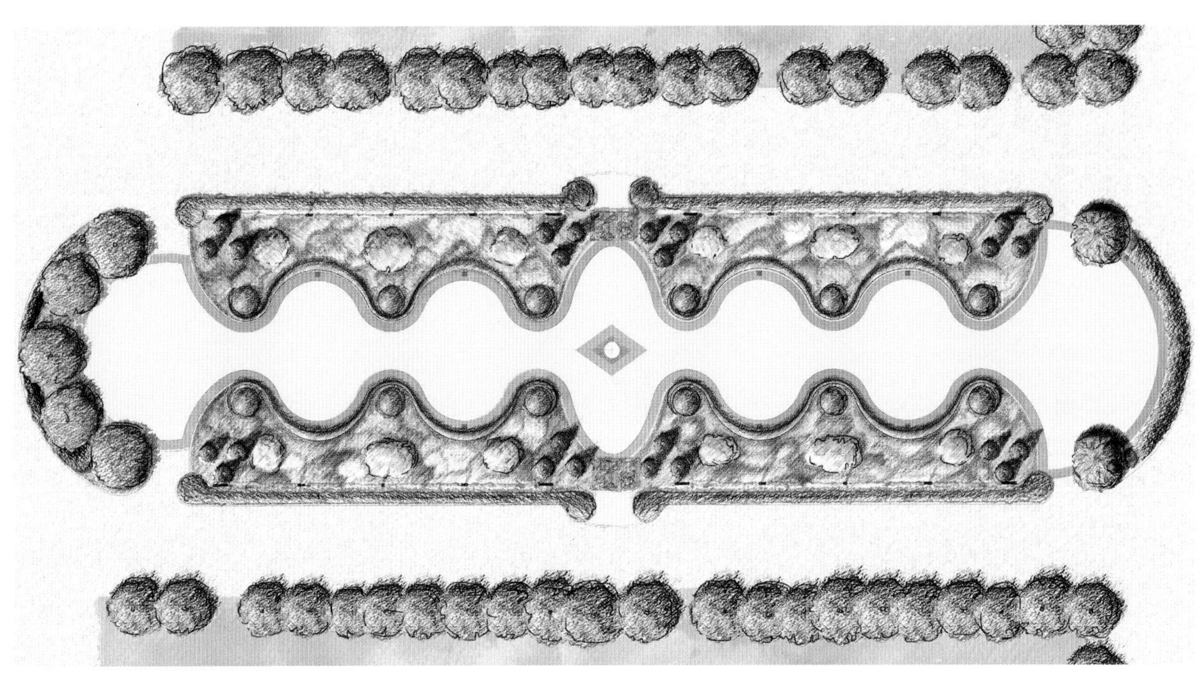

**During a quiet interval between festivities, OPPOSITE, the garden shows off the evergreen splendor and exalted view that give it four-season allure. Tall arborvitae (*Thuja occidentalis* 'Emerald Green') stand at attention behind stout yews (*Taxus* x *media* 'Fairview') and curlicues of boxwood. The baroque ins and outs of the axial plan, ABOVE, dramatize the spaces they clasp without detracting from the vista of Buckingham Fountain and Chicago's skyscrapers.**

scheme of whites, pinks, blues, and purples—set off by silver leaves—that climaxes late in the growing season with dahlias, butterfly bush, and sweet autumn clematis. After hard frosts prompt the exit of lingering blooms and foliage, their supporting players—evergreen box, arborvitae, and yews—take center stage. And when snow spotlights this majestic ensemble, it is a moment for living architecture to shine.

Ropes along side aisles are as graceful catching snowflakes, OPPOSITE, as they are bearing swags of the wisteria and sweet autumn clematis that ascend from summertime beds of nicotiana, ageratum, artemisia, phlox, and hydrangea, BELOW.

# Project Credits

Garden in the Round
Lake Forest, Illinois
Hoerr Schaudt: Douglas Hoerr
Landscape Contractor: Mariani Landscape
Masonry: Masonry by Fernando
Photographer: Scott Shigley

Renker Residence
Indian Wells, California
Hoerr Schaudt: Douglas Hoerr, Steven Gierke, Michael Ciccarelli
Interiors: Tom Stringer, Tom Stringer Design Partners
Landscape Contractor: Royal Landscape in Calabassas, CA
Photographers: Jack Coyier, Steven Gierke



Lake Michigan Estate
Chicago's North Shore
Hoerr Schaudt: Douglas Hoerr, John Evans
Architect: Randy Correll, Robert A.M. Stern Architects
Landscape Contractor: Mariani Landscape
Masonry: Masonry by Fernando
Photographers: Linda Oyama Bryan, Peter Aaron/OTTO for Robert A.M. Stern Architects

Crate & Barrel–Michigan Avenue Store
Chicago, Illinois
Hoerr Schaudt: Douglas Hoerr, Steven Gierke
Architect: Solomon, Cordwell, Buenz, and Associates
Photographers: Scott Shigley, Linda Oyama Bryan

Michigan Avenue Streetscape
Chicago, Illinois
Hoerr Schaudt: Douglas Hoerr, John Evans, Steven Gierke, Patrick Peterson
Landscape Contractor: Clarence Davids & Company
Photographers: Charlie Simokaitis, Steven Gierke, HSLA staff

Daley Plaza
Chicago, Illinois
Hoerr Schaudt: Peter L. Schaudt
Architect: DKL Architecture
Engineer: McDonough Associates, Inc.
Photographer: Martin Konopacki

Apple Stores
Chicago, Illinois
Hoerr Schaudt: Douglas Hoerr, Peter L. Schaudt
Architect: Peter Bohlin, Bohlin Cywinski Jackson
Photographers: Scott Shigley, Shigeyo Henriquez Studio

Buckhead Atlanta
Atlanta, Georgia
Hoerr Schaudt: Douglas Hoerr, John Evans, Michael Skowlund
Design Architects: Pappageorge Haymes Partners, Gensler
Architect of Record: Smallwood, Reynolds, Stewart, Stewart
Developer: Dene Oliver, OliverMcMillan, LLC
General Contractor: Balfour Beatty Construction
Photographer: Scott Shigley

North Park University
Chicago, Illinois
Hoerr Schaudt: Douglas Hoerr, John Evans, Shawn Weidner
Architect: Paul Hansen and William Ketcham, VOA
Landscape Contractor: Burkhart & Kinsella
Photographer: Scott Shigley

Dwarf Conifer Garden, Chicago Botanic Garden
Glencoe, Illinois
Hoerr Schaudt Staff: Douglas Hoerr, John Evans
Photographers: Chicago Botanic Garden/Robin Carlson, Linda Oyama Bryan

Soldier Field
Chicago, Illinois
Hoerr Schaudt: Peter Schaudt, Stephen Prassas, Jessica Ortega
Design Architect: Wood/Zapata Architecture
Architect of Record: Lohan Caprile Goettsch Architects
Photographer: Martin Konopacki

Lincoln Park Villa
Chicago, Illinois
Hoerr Schaudt Staff: Douglas Hoerr, Steven Gierke
Architect: Laurence Booth, Booth Hansen & Associates
Interiors: Arlene Semel and Brian Snow, SemelSnow Interior Design, Inc.
General Contractor: Tip Top Builders
Landscape Contractor: Mariani Landscape
Masonry: Masonry by Fernando
Photographers: Scott Shigley, Doug Snower

NoMi, Northern Michigan Home
Harbor Springs, Michigan
Hoerr Schaudt: Douglas Hoerr, Simon Prunty
Architect: Steve Rugo, Rugo/Raff Ltd. Architects
Interiors: Tom Stringer, Tom Stringer Design Partners
General Contractor: Jeff Ford, Evening Star Joinery
Landscape Contractor: Litzenburger Landscape
Photographers: Henry Joy IV, Hoerr Schaudt Staff

Classical Walled Garden
Chicago, Illinois
Hoerr Schaudt: Douglas Hoerr, John Evans, Shawn Weidner
Architect: Laurence Booth, Booth Hansen & Associates
Interiors: Roger Ramsay + Michael Syrjanen
General Contractor: Harold O. Schulz Company, Inc.
Landscape Contractor: Mariani Landscape
Photographer: Scott Shigley

Private Residence (page 86)
Lake Forest, Illinois
Hoerr Schaudt: Douglas Hoerr, Michael Ciccarelli
Architect: Rugo/Raff Ltd. Architects
Interiors: Athalie Derse, Inc.
Landscape Contractor: Mariani Landscape
Water Feature: Boilini Company
Masonry: Lake Forest Masonry
Photographer: Scott Shigley

Prairie Summer Home (page 87)
Harbor Springs, Michigan
Hoerr Schaudt: Douglas Hoerr, Simon Prunty
Interiors: Tom Stringer, Tom Stringer Design Partners
Landscape Contractor: Litzenburger Landscape
Photographer: Charles Mayer

Private Residence (page 88)
Wheaton, Illinois
Hoerr Schaudt: Douglas Hoerr
Architect: Laurence Booth, Booth Hansen & Associates
General Contractor: Arvid Eiesland, Eiesland Builders, Inc.
Photographer: Linda Oyama Bryan

Private Residence (page 89)
Michigan City, Indiana
Hoerr Schaudt: Douglas Hoerr, Michael Ciccarelli
Architect: David Woodhouse Architects
Interiors: Mitchell Putlack Interiors
General Contractor: Carlson Builders
Landscape Contractor: Gunner Piotter, Green Mansions
Photographer: Linda Oyama Bryan

Classical Walled Garden (page 90)
Chicago, Illinois
Hoerr Schaudt: Douglas Hoerr, John Evans, Shawn Weidner
Architect: Laurence Booth, Booth Hansen & Associates
Interiors: Roger Ramsay + Michael Syrjanen
General Contractor: Harold O. Schulz Company, Inc.
Landscape Contractor: Mariani Landscape
Photographer: Scott Shigley

Private Residence (page 92)
Chicago, Illinois
Hoerr Schaudt: Douglas Hoerr, Tiffany Evans
Architect: Dirk Denison Architects
General Contractor: Tip Top Builders
Landscape Contractor: Mariani Landscape
Photographer: Michelle Litvin

Private Residence (page 93)
Lake Geneva, Wisconsin
Hoerr Schaudt: Douglas Hoerr
Architect: Chip von Weise
Interiors: Suzanne Lovell
General Contractor: John Engerman, Engerman Companies
Landscape Contractor: Sheldon Landscape
Photographer: Doug Snower

Morningstar, Inc.
Chicago, Illinois
Hoerr Schaudt: Douglas Hoerr, Simon Prunty
Photographer: Scott Shigley

Ball Horticultural
West Chicago, Illinois
Hoerr Schaudt: Douglas Hoerr, John Evans, John Ware, Simon Prunty
Architect, Garden Pavilion: David Woodhouse Architects
Landscape Contractor: Clauss Brothers, Inc.
Photographers: Linda Oyama Bryan, Hoerr Schaudt Staff

Gary Comer Youth Center
Chicago, Illinois
Hoerr Schaudt: Peter L. Schaudt
Architect: John Ronan Architects
Photographer: Scott Shigley

Uptown Normal Circle
Normal, Illinois
Hoerr Schaudt: Peter L. Schaudt, Rob Gray
Architect: Doug Farr, Farr Associates
Engineer: Clark Dietz
Photographer: Scott Shigley
Special Thanks to Wayne Aldrich and Mercy Davisson

SandRidge Energy Commons
Oklahoma City, Oklahoma
Hoerr Schaudt: Peter L. Schaudt, Michael Skowlund, John Ridenour
Architect: Rogers Partners Architects
Photographers: Scott Shigley, Timothy Hursley

New England Farm
Portsmouth, Rhode Island
Hoerr Schaudt: Douglas Hoerr, Nicholas Fobes
Barn Architect: Eric J. Smith
Interiors: John Peixinho, Tom Scheerer
General Contractor: Kristy Perkins Construction
Landscape Contractor: Mike DaPonte, DaPonte Landscaping
Photographer: Scott Shigley

Island Retreat
Antigua, West Indies
Hoerr Schaudt: Douglas Hoerr, Steven Gierke, Abigale Baldwin
Architect: Colin Robinson
Interiors: Tom Scheerer, Tom Scheerer Inc.
General Contractor: Mount Joy Development
Landscape Contractor: Tropiscapes Limited
Lighting: Perry Kuhn, PCL Lighting
Photographers: Michael Stavaridis, Steven Gierke

900 North Michigan Avenue
Chicago, Illinois
Hoerr Schaudt: Douglas Hoerr, John Evans, Simon Prunty
Architect: Laurence Booth, Booth Hansen
General Contractor: Linn-Mathes
Landscape Contractor: Moore Landscapes
Photographers: Scott Shigley, Hoerr Schaudt Staff

McGovern Centennial Gardens
Houston, Texas
Hoerr Schaudt: Douglas Hoerr, Patrick Peterson, Katie Martin
Architect: Peter Bohlin, Bohlin Cywinski Jackson
Client/Project Management: Hermann Park Conservancy
Local Landscape Architect: White Oak Studio
General Contractor: Tellepsen Builders
Photographers: Terry Vine, Scott Shigley, Jim Wiehoff/Lifted Up Aerial Photography

Usher-Lambe Residence
Palm Springs, California
Hoerr Schaudt: Douglas Hoerr, Steven Gierke, Simon Prunty
Architect: Laurence Booth, Booth Hansen & Associates
Landscape Contractor: Tesera Outdoors
Photographer: David Blank Photo

Cascade House
Chicago's North Shore
Hoerr Schaudt: Douglas Hoerr, Simon Prunty, Steven Gierke
Architect: Peter Gluck, Gluck+
General Contractor: Jim True, ARC Construction
Landscape Contractor: Mariani Landscape
Masonry: Masonry by Fernando
Photographer: Scott Shigley

Bissell Residence
Grand Rapids, Michigan
Hoerr Schaudt: Douglas Hoerr, Tiffany Evans, John Evans
Architect: Rugo/Raff Ltd. Architects
Interiors: Phase I–Leslie Jones, Phase II–Tom Stringer, Tom Stringer Design Partners
General Contractor: Vandermale Builders
Landscape Contractor: Tom Rook, Rooks Landscaping
Lighting: Lightscape, Inc.
Photographer: Scott Shigley

Trump International Tower
Chicago, Illinois
Hoerr Schaudt: Peter L. Schaudt, Jessica Ortega
Architect: Skidmore, Owings & Merrill
Photographers: Scott Shigley, Okrent Associates

Greater Des Moines Botanical Garden
Des Moines, Iowa
Hoerr Schaudt: Douglas Hoerr, Nicholas Fobes
Architect: Michael Simonson, Simonson & Associates
General Contractor: The Weitz Company
Landscape Contractor: Country Landscapes, Inc.
Fountain Engineer: Delta Fountains
Lighting: Lightscape, Inc.
Photographer: Scott Shigley

Renker Garden
Harbor Springs, Michigan
Hoerr Schaudt: Douglas Hoerr, Simon Prunty, Steven Gierke
Architect: Steve Rugo, Rugo/Raff Ltd. Architects
Interiors: Tom Stringer, Tom Stringer Design Partners
General Contractor: Jeff Ford, Evening Star Joinery
Landscape Contractor: Litzenburger Landscape
Photographers: Scott Shigley, Steven Gierke

Botany Pond, University of Chicago
Chicago, Illinois
Hoerr Schaudt: Douglas Hoerr, Patrick Peterson
Planner: Richard Bumstead, University of Chicago
Photographer: Linda Oyama Bryan

Country Retreat
Highland Park, Illinois
Hoerr Schaudt: Douglas Hoerr, Nicholas Fobes
Architect: H. Gary Frank
General Contractor: Rocco DeFilippis
Landscape Contractor: Mariani Landscape
Masonry: Lake Forest Masonry
Landscape Restoration Consultant: Stephen Christy
Gardener, Property Manager: Tom Martin
Photographer: Scott Shigley

University of Chicago Main Quadrangle + Walkways
Chicago, Illinois
Hoerr Schaudt: Peter L. Schaudt, Jon Brooke
Project Representative: Richard Bumstead, University of Chicago
Civil Engineer: HOH Engineers
Photographer: Linda Oyama Bryan

Garfield Park Conservatory
Chicago, Illinois
Hoerr Schaudt: Douglas Hoerr, John Evans, Simon Prunty
Landscape Contractor: Clauss Brothers
Photographer: Shigeyo Henriquez Studio

IIT Campus
Chicago, Illinois
Hoerr Schaudt: Peter L. Schaudt
Architect, State Street Village: Helmut Jahn, Murphy Jahn Inc.
Lead Landscape Master Planner: Michael Van Valkenburgh
Photographers: Martin Konopacki, Leslie Schwartz, Richard Barnes, Yukio Futagawa
Vintage Aerial Photo: Courtesy University Archives & Special Collections, Paul V. Galvin Library, IIT

Chervon International Trading Company
Nanjing, China
Hoerr Schaudt: Peter L. Schaudt
Architect: Perkins+Will
Photographer: Steinkamp Photography

Cascade House Driveway
Winnetka, Illinois
Hoerr Schaudt Staff: Douglas Hoerr, Simon Prunty, Steven Gierke
Landscape Contractor: Mariani Landscape
Photographers: Steven Gierke, Scott Shigley, Linda Oyama Bryan

Nathan Phillips Square, The Podium
Toronto, Canada
Hoerr Schaudt: Peter L. Schaudt, John Ridenour
Architects: PLANT Architect, Inc., Perkins+Will Canada
Designer (site elements): Adrian Blackwell Urban Projects
Photographer: Chris Evans

Bank of America Stadium
Charlotte, North Carolina
Hoerr Schaudt: Peter L. Schaudt, Michael Skowlund, Patrick Peterson
Photographer: Scott Shigley

Rush University Medical Center
Chicago, Illinois
Hoerr Schaudt: Peter L. Schaudt, Patrick Peterson
Architect: Perkins+Will
Photographer: Steve Hall, Hedrich Blessing

A Photographer's Garden
Winnetka, Illinois
Hoerr Schaudt: Douglas Hoerr, Simon Prunty, Tiffany Evans, Patrick Peterson
Architect: Laurence Booth, Booth Hansen & Associates
Interiors: Arlene Semel and Brian Snow, SemelSnow Interior Design, Inc.
Landscape Contractor: Mariani Landscape
Builder: Arvid Eiesland, Eiesland Builders, Inc.
Photographers: Scott Shigley, Kate Joyce

Tiffany Celebration Garden
Chicago, Illinois
Hoerr Schaudt: Douglas Hoerr, Grace Rappe
Landscape Contractor: Jim Stevenson, Clauss Brothers, Inc.
Clients: Chicago Park District, Tiffany & Co.
Photographers: Steven Gierke, Linda Oyama Bryan